Continental
Air Defense

The CSIA Occasional Papers are a series of monographs sponsored by the Center for Science and International Affairs and co-published with University Press of America.

The Center for Science and International Affairs (CSIA) was established in 1973 to advance understanding and resolution of international security problems through a program of research, training, teaching, and outreach. Founded by Paul Doty, a biochemist long involved in arms control, national security, and science policy, CSIA became in 1978 the first permanent research center of Harvard's John F. Kennedy School of Government. The Center places special but not exclusive emphasis on the role of science and technology in the analysis of international security affairs.

Each year the Center hosts a multi-national group of scholars from the social, behavioral, and natural sciences. It sponsors seminars and conferences, many open to the public, and maintains a substantial specialized library in international security affairs. The Center also edits and sponsors the quarterly journal *International Security*, and publishes a working paper series as well as these Occasional Papers.

CSIA Occasional Papers
Available from UPA

No. 1, 1987.　Herbert York (with contributions by Albert Carnesale, Ashton Carter, George Rathjens, and Stephen Rosen). *Does Strategic Defense Breed Offense?*

No. 2, 1987.　Peter Stein and Peter Feaver. *Assuring Control of Nuclear Weapons: The Evolution of Permissive Action Links.*

No. 3, 1988.　Richard N. Haass. *Beyond the INF Treaty: Arms, Arms Control, and the Atlantic Alliance.*

No. 4, 1989.　Thomas W. Graham. *American Public Opinion on NATO, Extended Deterrence, and Use of Nuclear Weapons: Future Fission?*

No. 5, 1989.　Stephen D. Biddle and Peter D. Feaver, eds. *Battlefield Nuclear Weapons: Issues and Options.*

No. 6, 1990.　Graham T. Allison, Robert D. Blackwill, Albert Carnesale, Joseph S. Nye, Jr., and Robert P. Beschel, Jr., eds. *A Primer for the Nuclear Age.*

No. 7, 1990.　Arthur Charo. *Continental Air Defense: A Neglected Dimension of Strategic Defense.*

No. 8, 1990 (forthcoming).　Ivan Oelrich. *Conventional Arms Control: The Limits and Their Verification.*

No. 9, 1990 (forthcoming).　Bruce J. Allyn, James G. Blight, and David A. Welch, eds. *Proceedings of the Moscow Conference on the Cuban Missile Crisis, January 27–28, 1989.*

CSIA Occasional Paper No. 7

Continental Air Defense

A Neglected Dimension of Strategic Defense

By Arthur Charo

With an introduction by Ashton B. Carter

Published in cooperation with the Canadian Institute for International Peace and Security

Center for Science and International Affairs
Harvard University

Copyright © 1990 by the
President and Fellows of Harvard College

University Press of America®, Inc.
4720 Boston Way
Lanham, Maryland 20706

Henrietta Street
London WC2E 8LU England

Co-published by arrangement with the
Center for Science and International Affairs,
Harvard University

Library of Congress Cataloging-in-Publication Data

Charo, Arthur
Continental air defense : a neglected dimension of strategic
defense / Arthur C. Charo.
p. cm. — (CSIA occasional paper ; no. 7)
Includes bibliographical references.
1. United States—Air defenses, Military.   2. North America—Air
defenses, Military.   I. Title   II. Series.
UG733.C49   1990
358.4'145'0973—dc20   90-33480
CIP
ISBN 0-8191-7781-4 (University Press of America : alk. paper). —
ISBN 0-8191-7782-2 (University Press of America :
pbk. : alk. paper)

The paper used in this publication meets the minimum requirements of
American National Standard for Information Sciences—Permanence
of Paper for Printed Library Materials, ANSI Z39.48–1984.

CONTENTS

Tables

Figures

FOREWORD

Continental air defense has been a joint U.S.-Canadian responsibility for more than forty years. Neither country could pursue a study of it adequately without the other's collaboration. The Canadian Institute for International Peace and Security and its former Executive Director, Ambassador Geoffrey Pearson, co-sponsored with the Center for Science and International Affairs a major international conference on the subject at Harvard on February 12–13, 1988. This conference brought together U.S. and Canadian experts from government, industry, academia, and the armed services to discuss North American air defense modernization and the role of air defenses in continental security. Colleagues from CIIPS and CSIA and the participants at the conference aided enormously in the preparation of this Occasional Paper. In particular, Dr. Arthur Charo of CSIA and Professor David Cox of Queens University (formerly Director of Research at CIIPS) co-organized the conference. Professor Cox authored the section on "The Canadian Role in NORAD" in Chapter 1. However, CIIPS and the conference participants bear no other responsibility for the facts or judgments presented here.

Publication of this study would not have been possible without the professional attention of Ms. Lynn Whittaker, former Executive Director of CSIA, and Ms. Teresa Johnson, Assistant Managing Editor of *International Security*. Ms. Whittaker and Ms. Johnson accomplished the difficult task of editing a complex and highly technical manuscript. We are grateful to them for their contributions.

> —Joseph S. Nye, Jr., Director
>   Center for Science and International Affairs
> —Bernard Wood, Director
>   Canadian Institute for International Peace and
>   Security

AUTHOR'S
ACKNOWLEDGEMENT

It is a pleasure to have the opportunity to thank some of the many people who have contributed to this work. Ashton B. Carter, CSIA's Associate Director, was a constant source of encouragement and guidance during my residence at the Center. I feel fortunate to have had the opportunity to work with him, and am grateful for his critical review of earlier drafts of this manuscript. I would also like to thank the Social Science Research Council for supporting my research by awarding me a MacArthur Foundation Fellowship in International Security.

I benefited from the comments of many of my colleagues at CSIA, especially Lynn Eden, Dan Fenstermacher, Steve Fetter, Barry Fridling, and Steve Van Evera. Dan Hayward, formerly with Canada's Center for Arms Control and Disarmament, was an important source of information on Canadian defense policy.

Much of the inspiration for this Occasional Paper came from a CSIA-CIIPS conference on strategic air defense that I organized with Professor David Cox of Queens University, Canada. The success of the conference, (like NORAD), owes much to the cooperation and support of its Canadian participants. The conference attracted a superb group of experts on air defense, in large part due to the assistance of Caz Zraket from the MITRE Corporation; Bill Delaney from Lincoln Lab; Jack Ruina from MIT; Ash Carter and Joe Nye from CSIA, and Geoffrey Pearson of CIIPS. This paper draws on the expertise that was assembled at the conference, but in no way purports to represent the views of any of the individuals who participated.

The conference ran smoothly, despite Boston's biggest snowfall of the winter, thanks to Lynn Whittaker and Sofia Mortada of CSIA. I was fortunate to have the assistance of three excellent conference rapporteurs: John Lepingwell, Kerry Abelson, and Jane Boulden. John Lepingwell also helped organize the conference's session on Soviet strategic air defense. The role of air defense in Soviet strategic defense was discussed at the conference, but could not be included in this paper. Readers may wish to examine Lepingwell's "Soviet Strategic Air Defense and the Stealth Challenge," *International Security*, Vol. 14, No. 2 (Fall 1989), pp. 64–100.

The editing and production of this manuscript would not have been possible without the tireless efforts of CSIA's publications group. Lynn Whittaker helped in the earlier drafts; her responsibilities were later taken up by Teresa Johnson. I will always be grateful to Teresa for finally "getting air defense out the door." I would also like to thank Mike Stafford, Executive Director of CSIA, for his help with Chapter 5.

Last, I would like to thank my wife, Maude Fish, who adopted the cause of air defense and even initiated her own "Strategic Bassoon Initiative".

INTRODUCTION

By Ashton B. Carter

One claim the Strategic Defense Initiative has never made is to live up to its full title, although it has changed its stated purpose many times in its short lifetime. The SDI focuses exclusively on active defense against ballistic missiles, whereas the mission of "strategic defense" against nuclear attack properly includes two other ingredients: active defenses against bombers and cruise missiles (air defense), and passive defenses.

Passive defense of population, i.e., civil defense, is not much practiced in North America. But passive defenses of military targets are the foundation of strategic deterrence today, since they and they alone ensure the survival of retaliatory forces. Submarines hide in the ocean, command posts hide on land and in the air, bombers stand ready to escape their bases before attacking warheads can arrive, and the land-based missile huddles in its inadequately hardened silo awaiting a better basing mode.

SDI proposes to add active defenses against ballistic missiles to today's passive defenses. Adopting SDI in its most comprehensive vision—active defense of all of North America—would logically require adding an air defense "wall" to SDI's missile defense "roof." Air and missile defense would in any event have to depend on one another, the air defense for protection from suppression by missile attack, and the missile defense ground-based components for protection from air attack. And yet the SDI's budget is more than twenty-five times that of the Defense Department's Air Defense Initiative, and SDI gets almost all the public attention. More paradoxical still, the United States and Canada are jointly operating an air defense of North America at an annual cost in excess of $1 billion, whereas there is no missile defense of the continent whatsoever.

In this CSIA Occasional Paper, Dr. Arthur Charo, a physicist and former research fellow at CSIA, now Senior Analyst in the International Security and Commerce Program at the U.S. Congressional Office of Technology Assessment, gives to air defense the kind of technical and military analysis that missile defense has received at the hands of many analysts since the SDI was announced by President Reagan in 1983. Charo's analysis is meant to inform the current debates in the United States and Canada over the planned modernization of North American air defenses and the role that air defenses play in strategic defense. His analysis reveals several other reasons for taking a fresh look at continental air defense besides the prominence of its close cousin, the SDI. For one thing, the possibility that advancing technology will give defense a better chance against the nuclear offense than it has had to date is as worthy of study in air defense as it is in missile defense. Charo surveys emerging air defense technologies, from space-based radars to long-range interceptors.

Arrayed against these emerging defensive technologies are new offensive technologies, contending in a pattern of measure and countermeasure familiar from

discussions of SDI. In particular, the new long-range
Soviet cruise missiles and the inevitable emergence of
some form of "Stealth" techniques in the Soviet air-
breathing arsenal will challenge the ability of U.S.-
Canadian air defenses to continue to perform the relatively modest air defense tasks they perform today, let
alone to take on more ambitious tasks.

Interest in air defense should also grow in propor-
tion to the growth of the importance of air offense
within the strategic arsenals of both superpowers. Deep
missile cuts in the START agreement would leave a
larger fraction of the deterrent to air-breathing delivery
and would also reduce the number of missile warheads
available to suppress air defenses. Proposed counting
rules for penetrating bombers in START also invite a
buildup in air-breathing warheads. And in a development seemingly independent of arms control, the Soviet
Union is balancing its strategic triad with a newer and
larger air-breathing leg. The potential importance of
air defense grows correspondingly.

The ABM Treaty has banned missile defenses since
1972, but air defenses are completely unconstrained by
agreement. Why? And many, including the Soviet
START negotiators, maintain that offensive missile
agreements are incompatible with SDI. Yet agreements
have consistently included limits on air-breathers. Why?

All of these factors have caused the defense com-
munities in the United States and Canada to renew their
attention to continental air defense. This Occasional
Paper was inspired by this heightened interest.

Most people recognize that whether an SDI system
"works" or not depends above all on the defensive job it
is asked to do. So too, as Charo makes clear, with air
defense. Some of the possible goals for a continental air
defense are similar to the various goals for SDI, but

some are quite different. In a taxonomy similar but not identical to Charo's, I identify nine possible missions for a continental air defense.

Mission 1: Defense against accidental launch has been put forward by desperate defenders of SDI, so we need to examine it. Is there such a thing as an accidental sortie of a manned bomber or cruise missile carrier? Presumably not. I guess an accidental SLCM launch has as much plausibility as an accidental SLBM launch. But, overall, I do not think there is much content to this mission.

Mission 2: Defense against potential future possessors of nuclear bombs. This mission makes more sense for air defense than for missile defense, since if Qadhafi or a terrorist got a fission bomb, he would be more likely to use a plane than an intercontinental ballistic missile to deliver it. The problems here are as much operational as technical. One needs all-azimuth, all-altitude coverage of the United States and Canada, including coverage against raids staged from nearby friendly countries using the techniques of drug smugglers. The threat does not include penetration aids, and the defense itself is not threatened with suppression. On the other hand, the attack takes place against a background of normal peacetime air traffic (unless it is announced in advance by the terrorists and civil aircraft are stood down). Identification of targets as hostile is a complication that plagues air defense but that is entirely absent for missile defense. Identification and warning are not enough for Mission 2; the aircraft must be shot down before it reaches North America. We must be willing to shoot in ambiguous situations, a reminder of KAL 007 and the Iranian Airbus incidents.

Mission 3 is to provide *"airspace sovereignty."* Documents and testimony in support of the North American

Aerospace Defense Command (NORAD) are replete with this phrase. But no one seems to know how to define it operationally, or what benefit it confers if you have it.

Mission 4 would provide *warning of air attack* without any effort to intercept the attackers. Insofar as warning of Soviet sneak air attack is concerned, there is no need to try for more than half an hour warning, since there would not be any more warning time than that for ballistic missile attack, and there might even be less. If there is no intention to intercept intruders, there is no need to detect them far away from potential targets, either. Whether the high false alarm rate that might well accompany a high detection rate can be tolerated depends on what actions commanders intend to take during the period of warning.

At a minimum, commanders would want to "flush" bombers, tankers, airborne command centers, and airborne communications relays from their airfields. These aircraft are susceptible to SLBM attack with warning times of ten minutes or so today. One would not want a sneak cruise missile attack to shorten that timeline further. Flushing aircraft is not an irreversible step like launch of ICBMs under attack, so it would not be catastrophic to have a false alarm. But frequent false alarms during peacetime would not be tolerated. If the Soviet attack did not take place out of the blue, but in the midst of, say, a conventional war that was already under way, all civil aircraft might be stood down, eliminating that background problem.

The problem of warning against cruise missile sneak attack is simplified if warning only needs to be provided for certain targets, not for the whole continent. Thus one might put a "picket fence" around Washington and around coastal SAC bases. A final question about the warning mission for air defenses is whether attack assessment as well as warning is desirable, and how coarse the assessment can be.

Next, let us turn to the various roles for strategic air defense in a nuclear war with the Soviet Union that depend on intercept of intruders, not just warning. Here there are several distinct possibilities.

Mission 5 would match the kind of *comprehensive or near-perfect "astrodome" protection* exhibited in the more extravagant SDI view-graphs. This is an interesting exercise. As with SDI, there are lots of exotic future possibilities for sensors and weapons: space-based radars and infrared sensors, various multistatic radar concepts, exotic acoustic and seismic detection, space-based lasers, and long-range boost-glide interceptors. There are many penetration notions, from low-observables and decoys to suppression. There are several layers: in the first phase, analogous to boost, you try to destroy the enemy airplane, ship, or submarine before it releases the cruise missiles it is carrying. In the second phase, you try to kill the cruise missiles in their "midcourse" flight, before they reach North America. In the third phase, you make a last-ditch point-defense stand around key targets.

Short of intercepting almost all of the Soviet air-breathers before they reached North America in a first strike, *Mission 6* simply aims for *doing well against a second strike*. The attack that must be intercepted would be smaller due to our preceding attack; suppression of our defense by Soviet missiles would be smaller due to destruction or delay of their missiles; and we would be well alerted. I add this mission, which has the objectionable feature of requiring a first strike in order for the defense to work, to my list not merely out of an artificial desire for completeness. To many, this was the key mission of continental air defense in the 1950s; many believe it is a key mission of Soviet air defenses today.

Mission 7: Some people simply talk about *denying the Soviets a free ride.* This phrase seems to mean conceding that the Soviets could overcome the defense, but figuring that deploying it would force them into an expensive penetration effort.

Mission 8: Next, there is much attention to the mission of *preventing the Soviets from making repeated raids* on North America in a protracted nuclear war, or from seeking out and destroying mobile or reconstituted forces and C³I (command, control, communications, and intelligence). This mission seems both difficult and rather esoteric.

Finally *(Mission 9),* there are *local or point defenses,* rather than area or continental coverage defenses, of selected targets. The targets most often nominated for such defense are withheld (reserve) silo-based ICBMs, elements of an SDI system that cannot defend themselves against air-breathers, and isolated enclaves containing reconstituted forces, C³, and mobile ICBMs.

Each of these nine possible air defense missions poses a quite different technical challenge, varying with the size, sophistication, and degree of surprise in the threat; with whether defense itself or only warning of attack is needed; with whether one assumes a missile defense is also deployed along with the air defense for mutual support; and so on. Although I did not include it in the list, one should also take note of the nation's need for tactical air defenses, which share the same technologies and tactics as strategic air defense. Last, true visionaries are worried about defenses against non-nuclear strategic attack.

A great strength of Charo's analysis is his careful distinction among these missions and their respective technical implications. Few easily bridge the gap between technology and strategic affairs. It is a pleasure to find in this Occasional Paper, and in Art Charo, such a rare union.

Chapter 1

THE EVOLVING ROLE OF CONTINENTAL AIR DEFENSE

   Air defense has long been the neglected dimension of strategic defense. During the 1950s, it was a program of utmost importance to U.S. and Canadian security. However, as the dominant Soviet threat shifted from long-range bombers to intercontinental ballistic missiles in the early 1960s, interest in air defense began a rapid decline.[1] Now, after more than two decades of quiescence, defense against bombers is receiving renewed attention. This change is a consequence of several recent developments, including the emerging Soviet cruise missile threat, developments in stealth technology, possible reductions in ballistic missiles, new surveillance and weapons technologies, the development of the Strategic Defense Initiative (SDI), and new issues in the U.S.-Canadian defense relationship.

   This monograph provides a historical overview and technical assessment of current air defense issues, and offers some guidelines for analyzing issues likely to dominate the debate in the future. This introductory chapter briefly surveys the history of U.S. strategic air defense and describes relevant aspects of the Reagan administration's strategic modernization program and the Air Defense Initiative (ADI). It concludes with a summary of the Canadian role in NORAD, the North American Aerospace Defense Command (formerly the North American Air Defense Command).

Variations in Levels of Support for U.S. Air Defense

In the 1950s, Soviet long-range bombers posed the only strategic threat to the U.S. mainland. Efforts to defend the continental United States (CONUS) in this period culminated in the deployment of an elaborately controlled air defense network of early warning radars, manned interception aircraft, and surface-to-air missiles intended to protect both urban-industrial areas and strategic retaliatory forces. By 1957, the United States and Canada had strung 78 Distant Early Warning (DEW) radars across Alaska and the Canadian Arctic along the 70th parallel to survey polar approaches to Canada and the United States. In addition, they had erected an electronic tripwire (the Mid-Canada Line) along the 55th parallel to confirm an attack, and an additional line of tracking radars (the Pinetree line) along the 50th parallel near the U.S.-Canadian border.

Coastal approaches were guarded by U.S. Navy radar ships, microwave radars mounted on elevated platforms (Texas Towers), and Air Force ground and airborne surveillance radars. U.S.-Canadian air defense cooperation was formalized in 1958 with the creation of a unique joint military command, the North American Air Defense Command, NORAD (later renamed the

North American Aerospace Defense Command). At one point, over 3,000 manned interceptors, 200 of them Canadian, and about 90 nuclear-tipped BOMARC and Nike surface-to-air missile (SAM) batteries were placed on Canadian and U.S. territory.

U.S. commitment to air defense throughout the 1950s was quite high. By 1960, over 200,000 members of the U.S. armed forces supported the air defense mission. At their peak in the mid-1950s, annual expenditures for strategic air defense research, development, and acquisition exceeded $10 billion (1990 dollars), a remarkable figure in the New Look era of constrained defense spending. Research in air defense led to spectacular technological spinoffs including magnetic core memory and digital computers, which were used in SAGE (semi-automatic ground environment), the digital computer-based controlling network of the air defense system.

Despite these high levels of expenditure and effort, it was recognized that air defenses could limit, but not prevent, the massive damage that would occur in a nuclear exchange. Aircraft attrition rarely exceeded a few percent per mission in World War II, but postwar defense of urban and industrial areas against large fission and thermonuclear weapons, carrying up to a million times the energy of conventional chemical explosives, would require attrition approaching 100 percent. Under these circumstances, the Strategic Air Command (SAC) force of long-range nuclear-capable aircraft, coupled with the doctrine of massive retaliation, remained the primary deterrent to a nuclear attack.[2]

In the 1960s and 1970s, the funding and mission of the air defense network were substantially curtailed due to several factors: the growing vulnerability of air defense assets to ballistic missile attack; intelligence projections of a Soviet ICBM (inter-continental ballistic missile) force numbering in the thousands, while numbers of intercontinental bombers (then about 150) remained steady or declined; and the poor cost-effectiveness of any strategic defense compared to civil defense. Secretary of Defense Robert McNamara outlined these reasons in his Draft Presidential Memoranda of the early 1960s.[3]

Air defense expenditures, which had started falling in the last years of the Eisenhower administration, continued to decline in real terms throughout the 1960s and the first half of the 1970s, dropping to levels that were only about 10 percent of their peak mid-1950s values. Force levels also dropped precipitously in this period. By 1981, the number of interceptor aircraft assigned to continental air defense had declined from the 2,612 of the early 1960s to 307, mostly assigned to the Air National Guard. (The later interceptors were much improved compared to earlier versions—their number remained roughly constant throughout the 1980s.) In addition, all SAM batteries had been removed from CONUS by 1981, and manpower assigned to air defense reduced from 207,000 to 37,000. Canada followed the U.S. lead in air defense reductions, shutting down the Mid-Canada line in 1965 and removing the BOMARC SAMs.

The diminished goals of air defense were formally recognized in the late 1960s when the U.S. defense budget showed severe cutbacks in vulnerable ground-based command and control (C^2) elements of the air defense system. Proponents of the cuts, including McNamara, argued that the resulting savings could be redirected to survivable command and control. Indeed, at that time the Air Force expected to acquire a force of

81 modern airborne warning and control system air-craft (AWACS), 43 of which were to be designated for continental air defense. An upgraded interceptor force of F-12s was also urged.[4]

In effect, McNamara had linked the fortunes of air defense to those of ballistic missile defense. Following that reasoning, air defense should have remained a dormant issue after the signing in 1972 of the ABM (anti–ballistic missile) treaty, which severely limited re-search and deployment of ballistic missile defense (BMD) systems. By the end of the decade, however, concerns about the nation's air defense capabilities were again being raised as some members of Congress and the Air Force focused on new air-breathing threats and the deteriorating capabilities of what remained of the nation's air defenses. (Air-breathers are those aircraft whose engines use the oxygen in the atmosphere for combustion, in contrast to rockets, which carry their own oxidant.) The existing system had gaps in its cov-erage, limited ability to detect low-flying bombers, and little or no ability to detect, let alone engage, cruise missiles, an emerging threat. The system was also be-coming increasingly expensive to maintain, especially the DEW line radars that had been built without the benefit of solid-state electronics. Modern radars could offer much longer mean time between failures, a partic-ularly important consideration for systems deployed in the Arctic.

Renewed interest in air defense was also fueled by changes in strategic doctrine. Refinements in defense guidance, beginning in 1974 with the emphasis of NSDM-242 (National Security Decision Memorandum) on limited nuclear options, and culminating in 1980 with PD (Presidential Directive) 59's requirement that the United States develop more flexible nuclear responses, including the ability to fight a nuclear war up to several months long, placed increased emphasis on the endurance of retaliatory forces and the command and control of strategic offensive forces. While most defense analysts and members of Congress continued to view a strategy of mutual assured destruction (MAD) as an inescapable consequence of the overwhelming dominance of modern nuclear offensive forces, some pressed ever more vigorously for the development of active and passive strategic defenses. Congressman Ike Skelton, for example, argued at a House Armed Services Committee hearing in July 1981:

> The causes of our frail air defense program go back about twenty years. In the 1960s our military strategy adopted the policy of deterrence and, accordingly, we began to dismantle our strategic or active defensive system. Air defense was one of the victims. . . . It is my belief that most Americans now reject the so-called mutually assured destruction theory. This MAD theory is part of the reason we began to dismantle our defensive systems such as air defense and civil defense. . . . A rejection of MAD means we can start renovating our defense strategies.[5]

Air Defense Modernization in the Reagan Years

Ronald Reagan campaigned in 1980 on a Republican platform that decried the Carter administration's defense policies. After taking office, President Reagan sought to reverse what his advisers called a "decade of neglect" of America's defense preparedness, by announcing in 1981 a strategic modernization program. Improvements in continental air defense were among the program's top priorities. In response to the president, the Air Force developed a master air defense plan that was presented to Congress in 1982. The modernization included upgrades in existing systems and a major new surveillance program—over-the-horizon backscatter (OTH-B) radar (discussed in Chapter 4). The other major programs fall into four categories.

Arctic Surveillance. The Arctic Surveillance programs were designed to modernize, close gaps, and provide improved low altitude coverage for a radar barrier from Alaska across the Canadian Arctic along the 70th parallel, and down the East Coast to Labrador. The DEW line radars are being replaced with a North Warning System (NWS). The SEEK IGLOO replacement of the Alaskan radars, begun in 1979, was completed during the Reagan years.

The primary function of the NWS is barrier surveillance. When completed, NWS will consist of an overlapping network of 13 long-range (optimally, 200 nautical miles [nm]) minimally attended radars (MARs) providing high altitude coverage to 100,000 feet, and 39 shorter-range (60 nm) unattended radars (UARs) that fill in the gaps of the MARs at low altitude. These radars are modern solid-state microprocessor-controlled systems designed to give high probability of detection with very low false alarm rates against aircraft-size targets. Each can determine the elevation, range, and azimuth of targets, whereas older systems often needed two radars: one for range and azimuth, and a separate height-finder. The $1.3 billion cost of NWS is shared by the United States (60 percent) and Canada (40 percent).

Joint Surveillance System. The primary purpose of the Joint Surveillance System, jointly supervised by the U.S. Air Force and the Federal Aviation Administration (FAA), is airspace sovereignty. The system consists of a chain of radars around the border of the United States, manned primarily by FAA civilian employees engaged in air traffic control. Air traffic data from the JSS is also fed into NORAD.

The JSS system contributes radar warning data to NORAD, but its performance is limited by the small number of radar sites. Radar coverage is nearly continuous above an altitude of 10,000 feet, but there are gaps at low altitudes. In addition, JSS radars are not optimized for low-altitude detection since the radars are primarily designed for air traffic control of cooperative aircraft, not for detecting penetrating bombers or cruise missiles. Planned JSS upgrades include 40 new L-band radars at a cost of approximately $500 million, in addition to overall system improvements. The new radar network is expected to become operational in the mid-1990s.

Command and Control Upgrades. Air defense command and control has been consolidated into eight Region Operations Control Centers (ROCCs), which have replaced the older SAGE centers. The ROCCs supply data to NORAD, where all ballistic missile and air-breathing early warning data is processed. In crisis or wartime, the non-survivable ROCCs can be supplemented by the eight AWACS designated for CONUS defense, thus providing some defense since dispersal of AWACS and interceptors is planned. Atmospheric tactical warning and attack assessment also benefit from the $1 billion upgrade of C^3I, plant facilities, power supply, and computers underway at NORAD's Cheyenne Mountain complex.

New Interceptors. Fourteen air defense squadrons— two active and twelve National Guard—are located at sites around the periphery of the United States and Alaska. Alert aircraft are employed in response to radar detections to intercept and visually identify unknown intruders. These forces are controlled from the ROCCs, which process surveillance data.

The Air Force is modifying 270 of its F-16A and F-16B multi-role aircraft for some of the Air National Guard (ANG) fighter-interceptor squadrons that are currently equipped with F-106s, first deployed in the 1950s, and F-4C/Ds.[6] The F-16's most important improvement is its "look-down, shoot-down" capability, which enables it to detect low-flying targets and fire air-to-air missiles at them. The two active-duty squadrons, based in Alaska, and one of the twelve ANG units are equipped with F-15s, which also have look-down, shoot-down capability; the F-15's cost precluded its use to replace the ANG interceptors. The F-16 has a no-wind unrefueled mission radius greater than 850 nautical miles, according to General Dynamics. Modifications for the F-16s, begun in October 1988, will continue through February 1991.[7]

The F-16s are not new aircraft; they are being drawn from active Air Force squadrons as those squadrons are equipped with newer F-16C and F-16D aircraft. The cost of the air defense retrofit program is approximately $0.75 billion, not counting the costs of the aircraft being modified and the new-production F-16s that will replace those being shifted from other Tactical Air Command forces.[8]

In addition to these specific air defense modernization programs, President Reagan's vision of a world in which nuclear weapons are rendered "impotent and obsolete" revived a debate, arrested since the late 1960s, over the wisdom and technical feasibility of ballistic missile defense. Although NORAD's air defenses were slated for improvement at the time of the president's speech in March 1983, the total cost for all modernization items was orders of magnitude less than that estimated for ballistic missile defenses.[9] Even the improved air defense was admitted to have only a very limited capability to actually engage (i.e., intercept and shoot down) new air-breathing threats. Instead, the system's most important role was to support deterrence through improved warning capabilities.

Should the United States decide to deploy comprehensive ballistic missile defenses, a concurrent deployment of a vastly more expensive strategic air defense than the one now envisioned would be required to attempt to defeat air-breathing attacks on CONUS and to defend ground-based BMD components from follow-on air attacks. SDI deployment would be a compelling argument for *active* air defense. In addition, proponents of deterrence strategies that require an ability for protracted nuclear warfighting believe that an enduring air defense is necessary to defeat follow-on air attacks on reserve forces and surviving C³ (command, control, and communications). In particular, preserving a reserve force made up of mobile ICBMs such as Midgetman might require a mobile air defense.

The Air Defense Initiative

In July 1985 President Reagan directed the Department of Defense to begin the Air Defense Initiative (ADI).[10]

ADI is a research and development program that will assess future technology for all aspects of air defense against low-observable bombers and cruise missiles: surveillance, identification, tracking, and engagement, in both pre- and post-attack environments. Initially, the program was seen as a counterpart to SDI and was given the mission of evaluating system architectures for air defense on a timetable similar to that of SDI, that is, the early 1990s. ADI grew out of existing programs in cruise missile surveillance and atmospheric surveillance technology; to these were added battle management and cruise missile engagement technology. The widespread consolidation of BMD (ballistic missile defense) programs that occurred, especially with the establishment of the SDI Office (SDIO), has not taken place with ADI, which serves primarily to coordinate programs in the Department of Defense (DoD) and the services.[11] As a result, funding for ADI is only a small part of the total expenditure for air defense.

For the near future, ADI will focus on the development of advanced concepts and technologies applicable to the detection of cruise missiles and aircraft, both in their current versions and in future variants expected to have lower radar visibility. ADI is also investigating advanced active and passive sensors to track submarines or detect launch of SLCMs (sea-launched cruise missiles). ADI's major funding categories are shown in Table 1-1.

Despite ADI's initial charge, and subsequent reports in defense journals that it would "provide the walls for the SDI roof," ADI-SDI coupling appears to be loose.[12] While concepts for active defense are being explored in a preliminary way, the bulk of ADI's resources are being devoted to developing advanced surveillance systems. ADI officials clearly recognize that the development of

TABLE 1-1. ADI FUNDING (then-year U.S. dollars in millions).

	FY 87 Funding	FY 88 Funding	FY 89 Request[1]
Integration and Architecture			
Air Force	$ 3.5	$ 2.7	$ 15.2
Navy	0.0	5.0	5.2
Surveillance[2]			
Air Force	28.3	25.4	131.8
Navy	0.0	5.0	30.0
Engagement			
Air Force	0.5	0.5	12.0
Navy	0.0	2.0	5.0
Battle Management/C[3]			
Air Force	0.6	2.2	14.3
Classified Activities	0.0	6.4	28.0[3]
TOTAL	$32.9	$49.2	$213.5

SOURCE: ADI funding figures are from "Air Defense Initiative: Program Cost and Schedule Not Yet Determined," GAO/NSIAD-892FS (Washington, D.C.: U.S. General Accounting Office, 1988).

NOTES:
1. The FY 89 total request was funded at $157.4 million: $96.4 million to the Air Force, $33 million to the Navy, and $28 million to DARPA (Defense Advanced Research Projects Agency) for classified activities. The FY 90 request was $257.2 million. Robert C. Duncan, Director of Defense Research and Engineering, in letter to Frank C. Conahan, Assistant Comptroller General, National Security and International Affairs Division, U.S. General Accounting Office, February 24, 1989. The FY 1990 appropriation was approximately $150 million; as of March 1990, the Bush administration was seeking to increase FY 91 funding to $246.9 million.
2. In 1988, approximately half of ADI's surveillance budget was devoted to demonstration radar for the Advanced Surveillance Tracking System, a follow-on to AWACS designed to recoup the lost capability of AWACS against the current generation of low-observable targets. The ASTS program has since been renamed the Advanced Surveillance and Tracking Technologies program.
3. The FY 89 request for classified activities is not known; this figure represents actual funding. See sources cited in note 1.

engagement systems presupposes adequate surveillance; they are also wary of tying their program too closely to the erratic fortunes of SDI.

In the near term, most of the technological potential for ADI-SDI overlap appears to lie in battle management, C³ and surveillance technologies. Hypothetical applications of directed energy weapons to air defense are being discussed. However, the development of usable weapons for air defense appears to require systems with capabilities and development times similar to those envisioned for ballistic missile defense.

SDI's funding has dwarfed that of ADI. For FY (fiscal year) 1990, ADI received about four percent (or about $15. million) as much as the funding allocated to SDI. However, SDI faces an increasingly skeptical Congress, and continued support even at current funding levels has been jeopardized by the departure from office of SDI's greatest champion, President Reagan. Although ADI's funding is not likely to approach SDI's, concerns about the emerging cruise missile threat and the importance of air defense in conventional conflicts could conceivably give ADI and related air defense programs more stable funding and perhaps a more lasting influence, than SDI.

The Canadian Role in NORAD

U.S. and Canadian interservice cooperation in continental air defense, which had grown steadily in the 1950s, was formalized in 1958 with the establishment of NORAD, a bilateral command integrating the surveillance and active air defenses of the two countries. The decision to establish NORAD was controversial in Canada, its critics alleging that their government had failed to protect Canadian political independence and that the Royal Canadian Air Force (RCAF) was hand-in-glove with the U.S. Air Force (USAF). At frequent intervals thereafter, issues arose that rekindled the controversy. In the early 1960s, debate over the acquisition of U.S.-supplied nuclear weapons for Canadian air defense interceptors proved a highly political issue which contributed significantly to the demise in 1963 of the Progressive Conservative government. At the time of the 1968 NORAD renewal, there was considerable opposition in Canada to any involvement in ballistic missile defense. Canadian concerns were eased by a clause in the 1968 agreement that NORAD "would not involve in any way a Canadian commitment to participate in an active ballistic missile defense."

The original NORAD agreement was signed for ten years, to be renewed at five-year intervals. In 1973, however, uncertain about U.S. intentions for air defense modernization in the wake of the SALT I negotiations and the signing of the ABM Treaty, Canada requested a temporary two-year renewal pending clarification of U.S. plans. In 1974, Secretary of Defense James Schlesinger essentially confirmed the McNamara verdict of the mid-1960s by advising Congress that the objectives of air defense were to provide peacetime surveillance and control of airspace, to give warning of a bomber attack, and to provide a limited defense against a bomber attack when augmented with tactical air forces.

On balance comfortable with this approach, Canada renewed the agreement in 1975 with little domestic debate. In 1980, fulfilling a promise to permit a full parliamentary review, the agreement was temporarily renewed for one year, followed by a five-year renewal in

1981. Ironically, the clause explicitly exempting Canada from a commitment to participate in BMD was dropped from the 1981 agreement, ostensibly on the grounds that, in light of the ABM treaty, it was invidious to imply that the United States, as the senior NORAD partner, might be contemplating an ABM defense. In the aftermath of President Reagan's SDI speech of March 23, 1983, this point again became an issue of domestic concern in Canada, particularly after Secretary of Defense Caspar Weinberger's March 26, 1985, invitation to the NATO allies to participate in SDI research. The 1986 renewal of NORAD thus became the occasion for a full-scale review of the connections between SDI and continental air defense.

The issue around which the Canadian debate focused was the March 18, 1985, agreement between President Reagan and Prime Minister Brian Mulroney to develop the North Warning System (NWS) as the replacement for the DEW line. The U.S. Department of Defense, by the early 1970s, had settled on an air defense modernization program compatible with the goals of early warning and peacetime surveillance. This program called for the development of OTH-B radars, AWACS, an improved manned interceptor, and the creation of the joint surveillance system. For Canadian planners this posed two dilemmas. First, there was no specific plan to replace the DEW line: if a northern-based OTH-B was not technically feasible, the United States considered the solution to be AWACS flights across northern Canada. Second, as the Pinetree line became obsolescent, there was little U.S. interest in replacing it. The U.S. Air Force made it clear that, if Canada chose to modernize the Pinetree line, it would be seen as a national initiative rather than a contribution to NORAD.

For Canadian planners, the U.S. approach forced

consideration of air defense modernization. Without U.S. contribution to the maintenance and operation of the Pinetree line, renovating it was impractical; lacking the DEW line, Canada would lack basic surveillance of its territory and polar approaches. The problem was compounded by the dead areas of the OTH-Bs, which, extending 500 miles from OTH-B locations, meant that critical air approaches to Canada on its east and west coasts were not covered. In light of these concerns, Canadian planners took the initiative in proposing further cooperative studies, which resulted in the 1979 Joint U.S.-Canadian Air Defense Study (JUSCADS). From this study came both a proposal for an additional OTH-B in the central U.S. to cover the dead areas and, more important from the Canadian point of view, an agreement to build the NWS as an interim replacement for the DEW line.

At $1.3 billion, the NWS promised greater efficiency and lower operating costs, but like the DEW line it was a peacetime surveillance system with no capability to survive an attack. It represented, therefore, a clear choice to pursue a conventional, current-technology modernization program suitable for perhaps ten to fifteen years, rather than to wait for new systems which, in the JUSCADS approach, seemed likely to center on space-based radars.

The planning of the NWS thus had more to do with the decay of the radar systems of the 1950s than the new technologies of ballistic missile defense; nevertheless, the March 1985 agreement to proceed with NWS, itself seen as an achievement by Canadian defense planners, drew fire from two very different quarters. On the one hand, Arctic specialists complained that the line would not meet the requirement for comprehensive surveillance far north. The choice of locations, largely on existing DEW line sites, seemed to have been determined entirely by cost considerations. Surveillance and tracking over Canadian territory north of the NWS would thus require U.S. AWACS. Lacking funds to purchase and operate the four or five AWACS aircraft needed for adequate coverage of the northern areas, Canadian defense planners settled for an arrangement that permitted Canadian Air Force personnel to fly on U.S. AWACS aircraft, promised dispersed operating bases for AWACS in Canadian territory, and provided for communications improvements at North Bay to coordinate Canadian interceptors with AWACS operations. In addition to 40 percent of the cost of the NWS system, Canada is contributing forward operating locations and dispersed operating bases for fighter and AWACS operations, AWACS and OTH-B manning, and communications and radar station support and personnel.

Meanwhile from a quite different perspective of the debate, Canadian opponents of SDI complained that the NWS agreement was another element in the NORAD framework that would draw Canada inexorably into ballistic missile defense. While it was manifestly not the intention of Canadian defense planners who had promoted the NWS to associate it with SDI, the debate that took place over the 1986 renewal of NORAD identified an emerging contradiction in Canadian policy. The Progressive Conservative government had been cool to the Weinberger invitation to participate on a government-to-government basis in SDI research. While emphasizing the right of any Canadian company to bid on SDI contracts, the Conservative government sought to distance itself from the SDI program. Moreover, senior Cabinet ministers made strong statements on Canada's commitment to arms control, and in particular to the ABM treaty. However, as the JUSCADS study and the NWS decision had demonstrated to the satisfaction of defense planners, there were strong incentives for Canada to continue to cooperate in continental air defense.

This position was emphasized in the 1987 Defense White Paper, which announced that Canada would undertake research into future air defense systems "in conjunction with" the Air Defense Initiative. It also promised funds for research into space-based surveillance systems as a follow-on to the NWS. "Only space-based surveillance," noted the White Paper, "has the potential for complete coverage of Canadian territory and adjoining air and sea space."[13]

The U.S. Air Defense Initiative was designed to complement SDI so that the two programs could proceed in tandem. By contrast, since the Defense White Paper, Canada has appeared more committed than ever to the continental air defense partnership, while rejecting the arms control implications of any U.S. move to deploy ballistic missile defenses or to break out of the ABM treaty.

Notes

1. For detailed histories, see Joseph Jockel, "The United States and Canadian Efforts at Continental Air Defense, 1945–1957" (PhD dissertation, The Johns Hopkins University, 1978); Jack H. Nunn, "American Air Defense Developments" (unpublished Working Paper, Center for International Studies, MIT, 1980); and David Cox, *Canada and NORAD, 1958–1978: A Cautionary Retrospective*, Aurora Paper No. 1 (Ottawa: Canadian Center for Arms Control and Disarmament, 1985).

2. Even optimistic estimates of the effectiveness of continental air defenses in this period assumed that a sizeable fraction of Soviet bombers would reach their targets. Nevertheless, meaningful dam-

age limitation still seemed possible, according to participants in the air defense effort of the 1950s, because Soviet bomber forces were relatively small. Furthermore, since Soviet production of nuclear weapons was assumed to be at full capacity, the deployment of U.S. air defenses could not prompt an offsetting offensive response (a concern frequently expressed in the current debate over ballistic missile defenses). It was not until the 1960s that the ballistic missile emerged as both the primary means of nuclear weapons delivery and the ultimate weapon to suppress air defenses.

3. Robert McNamara, "Recommended FY 1966–1970 Programs for Strategic Offensive Forces, Continental Air and Missile Defense Forces, and Civil Defense (U)," Memorandum for the President, December 3, 1964.

4. The F-12 was never built, nor were AWACS procured on nearly as large a scale as then contemplated. Although eight AWACS aircraft are currently designated for continental air defense in wartime, their primary role, and the continuing procurement justification, is theater defense. In the United States, AWACS are assigned to the Tactical Air Command (TAC), reflecting both their primary mission and the greater procurement authority of TAC versus NORAD.

5. House Armed Services Committee (HASC) hearing on "Continental Air Defense," HASC No. 97–54, Full Committee Hearing on Continental Air Defense, July 22, 1981 (Washington, D.C.: U.S. Government Printing Office [U.S. GPO], 1982).

6. At one time Air Force officials considered replacing the aging F-106 air defense interceptors with converted F-4s, because the F-4 could carry the large radar set employed by the Air Force's most capable interceptor, the F-15. The decision to choose the F-16A remains controversial. On the F-16 upgrade, see "The Return of Air Defense," *Air Force Magazine*, October 1987, pp. 82–87; and "USAF Selects Modified F-16A as Air Defense Fighter," *Aviation Week and Space Technology*, November 10, 1986.

7. The F-16 is modified for air defense with two 600-gallon external fuel tanks, two radar-guided AMRAAMs (Advanced Medium Range Air-to-Air Missile), and two heat-seeking AIM-9 Sidewinder air-to-air missiles. Delays in the AMRAAM program have set back plans to deploy it as a successor to the AIM-7 radar-guided Sparrow.

8. "Aircraft Procurement: Air Force Air Defense Fighter Competition," GAO/NSIAD-86-170 BR (Washington, D.C.: U.S. General

Accounting Office [U.S. GAO], 1986), p. 7. The total cost for acquiring the 270 air defense fighters is estimated to be approximately $4 billion.

9. The cost for the modernization package (OTH-B radars, the NWS, USAF AWACS to supplement NWS at times of alert, forward locations and dispersed operating bases to be developed at existing Canadian airfields for AWACS and fighter aircraft, and communications equipment to facilitate command and control of the interceptors) is estimated at about $7 billion. From "Canada-U.S. Agreement on the North Warning System," in *A Guide to Canadian Policies on Arms Control, Disarmament, Defence, and Conflict Resolution 1985–86* (Ottawa: Canadian Institute for International Peace and Security, 1986). Canada's share of the cost of the air defense modernization is approximately $600 million (U.S. dollars). The bulk of this expenditure is slated for the North Warning System (Canada is contributing 40 percent of the acquisition cost). Not included in the $600 million is the purchase of 138 CF-18 interceptors, some of which are designated for an air defense role.

10. An analysis of ADI, including prospects for Canadian participation, appears in Daniel Hayward, *The Air Defense Initiative*, Issue Brief No. 9 (Ottawa: Canadian Centre for Arms Control and Disarmament, 1988).

11. ADI is managed by the Office of the Secretary of Defense (OSD), and is executed by the Air Force and the Navy. Within OSD, oversight for ADI comes from the Office of the Deputy Undersecretary for Strategic and Theater Nuclear Forces.

12. See, e.g., Jim Coghlan, "Countering the Cruise Missile," *Defense Electronics*, September 1987, pp. 77–86; and John D. Morrocco, "Push for Early SDI Deployment Could Spur Air Defense Initiative," *Aviation Week and Space Technology*, February 2, 1987, pp. 18–20.

13. Defense White Paper, "Challenge and Commitment: A Defense Policy for Canada" (Ottawa, Canada: Department of National Defence, 1987), p. 58.

Chapter 2

THE MISSIONS OF AIR DEFENSE

The foremost mission for strategic air defense should be to provide unambiguous warning of an incoming attack by bombers or cruise missiles. The most important objective of such warning is to gain time to protect those parts of the U.S. deterrent force that are vulnerable to such an attack, especially the strategic bomber and tanker force and the fleet of emergency command and communications aircraft.

Although it is most important, tactical warning is only one of the possible missions of air defense.[1] The missions of U.S. air defense fall into six categories: the first, air traffic control/airspace sovereignty, and second, tactical warning and attack assessment, are both recognized by the U.S. Air Force as explicit priorities. The third, preventing a Soviet "free ride," is achieved to some degree by resources devoted to the first two missions. It is suggested here that a fourth possible mission, defending against terrorist or small country attack, is impractical. The fifth and sixth are active defense missions: defense of selected deterrent forces (point defense), and damage limitation through nationwide defense. These exist only in a rough concept stage.

21

While the ordering of these missions is roughly from the simplest to the most difficult, the definition of success for any given mission is subject to considerable ambiguity. This chapter examines in some detail each of these missions and the requirements for performing them, giving most attention to the warning mission. It concludes with an assessment of similarities and differences between the missions of air defense and those of ballistic missile defense.

Air Traffic Control and Airspace Sovereignty

All commercial, private, and military aircraft approaching the United States or traveling within its boundaries are required to limit their flights to predesignated airspace corridors. Air traffic controllers are kept apprised of an aircraft's whereabouts through active radar interrogation and cooperative procedures that all aircraft are expected to obey. This peacetime regulation of movement—the air traffic control system—has as its goals the safety and timely transport of passengers and cargo.

In contrast to this well-defined mission, airspace sovereignty is a vague concept. Civilian and military officials agree on its importance, but rarely detail its requirements. Some would be satisfied with a "Coast Guard of the air"—a border patrol system that provides minimal peacetime surveillance of territorial airspace, perhaps with a small inspector force of interceptors. Others believe that nothing short of a system able both to detect and to identify every aircraft that penetrates territorial airspace is sufficient. A feeling that border control is essential to preserve nationhood underlies the emotional attachment to the sovereignty mission, especially in Canada.

An even more demanding view of sovereignty, one that aspired to *control* all territorial airspace against a determined intruder, would require detection, identification, and interception at all altitudes over the entire 14,000-kilometer perimeter of the continental United States, or the 21,000-kilometer perimeter of North America. Operationally, these requirements must be met in peacetime when the rules of engagement call for visual identification, a very demanding task.

The wartime missions of the North American air defense network would not necessarily require meeting the most demanding requirements of sovereignty. Indeed, wartime air defense systems might be optimally concentrated at locations of high strategic value or along likely penetration corridors, leaving some sovereign territory unprotected. Without a clear standard of reference, air defense expenditures for any mission may always be justified in part by their overlap with the systems needed for maintaining airspace sovereignty.

The Soviet Union, which maintains the world's most elaborate air defenses, has the control of territorial airspace as one of its primary air defense missions. Nevertheless, Soviet air defenses have seen several spectacular failures. In 1978, Soviet air defense forces failed to stop Korean Airlines Flight 902 as it crossed the border and flew over Murmansk. Later, contact was lost briefly as the aircraft flew over the heavily defended Kola Peninsula. This incident prompted high-level reviews of military operations and may have contributed to the military theater command reorganization that followed within a year. Despite these steps, in 1983 another Korean plane, Flight 007, twice penetrated Soviet airspace while flying at a cruising altitude of

33,000 feet. It first entered Soviet airspace over the sensitive Kamchatka Peninsula, but four interceptors (given incorrect coordinates by ground controllers) failed to locate the airliner before it reentered international airspace. KAL 007 was in Soviet airspace for extended periods taking no evasive action before it was finally destroyed by a Soviet interceptor that apparently violated Soviet rules of engagement by failing to confirm visually the identity of the aircraft.[2] In May 1987, Mathias Rust, a West German pilot in a single-engine Cessna, flew unimpeded from Hamburg over hundreds of miles of Soviet airspace before landing in Moscow's Red Square. While these failures do not mean that Soviet air defenses would not be formidable in wartime, they show that controlling airspace, even in peacetime and even with an elaborate air defense system, is a formidable task.

Tactical Warning and Attack Assessment

There is broad agreement in the U.S. defense community that the foremost mission of aerospace defense is assured warning—the detection and timely transmission of tactical warning of attack to military leaders and the National Command Authority (NCA).[3] Assessment of the size of the attack and its targets is also necessary to assist the NCA in choosing retaliatory options.

Assured warning is an essential component of both deterrence and crisis stability, since deterrence is based on a credible threat of retaliation, and crisis stability depends on minimizing incentives for preemptive attack even if an enemy appears poised to strike first. Assured warning is essential for deterrent strategies ranging from assured destruction to more ambitious damage-limiting strategies that rely on prompt response.

Early warning satellites and ground-based radar could detect an attack by Soviet ballistic missiles 15–30 minutes before warheads would arrive over U.S. targets. U.S. retaliatory forces are maintained in a state of readiness that permits authorities, during this period, to effect some or all of the following steps: 1) order aloft ("flush") the bombers, tankers, and airborne emergency command and communications aircraft (especially the Post-Attack Command and Control System fleet, PACCS)[4] that are maintained on 15-minute ground alert, in order to prevent their destruction on the ground, and disperse ground-mobile communication and command posts; 2) transfer control of the nuclear forces from vulnerable to invulnerable command centers; 3) launch ICBMs or other nuclear forces ("launch under attack" or LUA); and 4) disperse or launch mobile ICBMs (if the United States acquires a mobile missile force).[5]

At minimum, air defense warning sensors should provide the same amount of warning as ballistic missile early warning sensors, that is, 15 minutes before impact. Although the Air Force believes that enemy bomber-sized targets could not penetrate radar surveillance barriers undetected after modernization is finished in the early to mid-1990s, many analysts believe cruise missile detection will remain problematical. Surveillance of cruise missile *carriers*—bombers carrying ALCMs (air-launched cruise missiles) and submarines and surface ships carrying SLCMs (sea-launched cruise missiles)—is therefore essential. In particular, threat of SLCM attack implies that naval anti-submarine warfare (ASW) must become an important part of the plan for atmospheric surveillance.

Detecting the carrier is a necessary but not sufficient condition to carry out the warning mission. Suppose that during a superpower crisis, U.S. over-the-horizon radars detect several unknown aircraft 1,000 miles offshore, and that military authorities are reasonably certain that these aircraft are potentially hostile Soviet cruise missile carriers. How should the United States respond if it is not possible to detect the launch of a cruise missile? Although some survivability measures could be initiated, an extreme action such as flushing bombers would require balancing the dangers of not protecting retaliatory forces against the dangers of a false alarm. (Because sending bombers aloft is provocative, and "recycling" launched bombers makes them more vulnerable, this action has never yet been taken in a crisis.)

Warning has two components: detection of a target and verification that it is hostile. The air defense literature is full of technical innovations for improving surveillance and control systems. However, because an air attack must be distinguished from normal air traffic, the key to making full use of these innovations in peacetime is to develop reliable means for non-cooperative identification. Long-range or forward deployment of radar systems combined with visual identification by manned interceptor aircraft is only a partial and expensive solution to the problem. Unfortunately, no better solution exists at this time.

A long-range aircraft or cruise missile will typically travel less than 150 miles in 15 minutes. Therefore, early warning would not require long-range surveillance radars or forward deployed radars if assessment of air-breathing attack were as reliable as it is for ballistic missile attack. An alternative to wide-area surveillance is local surveillance at selected sites that are deemed essential to support the survivability measures listed earlier.

Attack assessment is the other part of the warning mission. For air attacks, assessment is complicated by the inability to determine in advance an aircraft or cruise missile's target. If, however, one believes that the small sneak attack, discussed next, is the only plausible use of air-breathers in a first strike, then attack assessment is relatively unimportant. The goal would be simply to recognize that an attack was in progress, and assume that its goal was to disrupt the response options listed above.

Warning and the Precursor Attack. The most worrisome attack scenario for air-breathing forces in a Soviet first strike is the "leading edge" or precursor attack—a small surprise attack designed to increase U.S. vulnerability to a larger disarming strike by ballistic missiles. In the past, this attack was dismissed by analysts who believed an attack by slow-moving bombers, liable to detection hours from their targets, would pose an unacceptable risk to Soviet planners. It is receiving renewed interest with the emerging threat from cruise missiles.

Underlying the plausibility of the precursor attack are the assumptions that: the Soviet Union seeks the capability to initiate large-scale nuclear attacks on the U.S. retaliatory forces (presumably to limit damage from an apparently imminent U.S. first strike); Soviet planners believe the weight of U.S. retaliation can be diminished by surprise attacks on the U.S. strategic C^3 network and bomber bases; and the low detectability of cruise missiles gives the Soviets a chance at surprise, that is, attack without tactical warning. These considerations would also apply to Soviet planners contemplating a precursor attack using submarine-launched ballistic missiles (SLBMs). As discussed below, the threat of the air-breathing precursor attack versus the SLBM precursor attack, the "standard" attack scenario, turns on the value of a few extra minutes of warning.

Precursor attacks on the U.S. C³ network would be designed to delay or confuse the U.S. decision-making chain and to disrupt ballistic missile early warning data. Primary targets might include Washington, D.C., other major command centers, satellite early warning system (SEWS) ground terminals, ballistic missile early warning system (BMEWS) ICBM radars, Pave Paws SLBM early warning radars, communication transmitters, SAC bomber and tanker bases, and air bases that house the PACCS and Worldwide Airborne Nuclear Command Post (WWABNCP) aircraft or their alternates. Secondary targets might include airfields with alert fighter and AWACS aircraft, and nuclear submarine bases if the enemy wants to eliminate even the small chance that SSBNs and SSNs in port do not escape the follow-on attack. An attack on all of these targets would be large and risky. Even a successful Soviet counterforce attack would leave the United States with thousands of warheads on SLBMs at sea.

An attack in normal peacetime on the NCA, the National Military Command Center, and the Alternate National Military Command Center (all in or near Washington, D.C.) is an obvious example of a very small but potentially high-leverage attack. At the other extreme, if U.S. forces and surveillance activities were on high alert, a precursor attack would need to be very large and would incur a substantially greater risk of detection. The logic of the precursor attack demands that preparations for the attack be disguised and the attack itself occur without giving the United States more than several minutes of tactical warning.

The distinction between coastal and inland targets is also important. During normal peacetime alert status,

SAC bombers and tankers are located at bases both near the U.S. coast and thousands of miles inland. Although the PACCS command and communication fleet is based inland, alternates to the TACAMO airborne submarine communication relay aircraft are routinely based near the coast (one TACAMO is always airborne off each of the east and west coasts, but they have limited endurance). Tactical Air Command and Air National Guard fighter-interceptors assigned to air defense are also based near the coast, as are submarines in port. U.S. ICBMs and the proposed areas for mobile missile deployment are both located inland, in the Midwest or Southwest.

For several reasons, a precursor attack would likely be confined to targets near the coast. First, the United States is surrounded by a long coastline where many important military targets, especially early warning, command, and communication sites, are located. Second, simultaneous attacks on *both* inland and coastal targets separated by hundreds of miles would create formidable timing and coordination problems; attacks that are not simultaneous would allow attack warning to be transmitted through undamaged portions of the C^3 network, defeating the purpose of the precursor attack. Bombers or cruise missiles, traveling at subsonic speed over land for hours, would also be more vulnerable to detection than weapons traveling shorter distances over water.

A precursor attack of SLCMs launched from submerged submarines may be the most plausible of the air-breathing attack scenarios because submarines are inherently stealthy and might be able to approach coastal targets without detection. The flight time of a long-range cruise missile is similar to ICBM flight time, 30 minutes, if launch occurs within 300 miles of the target. If launch occurs within 150 miles of a target, cruise missile flight times would be reduced to typical SLBM flight times (on normal trajectories). Short-range attacks might also allow use of supersonic cruise missiles to reduce flight times by a factor of two or more, although they are not a current Soviet SLCM option.

Even a SLCM attack poses some risk of detection. Unlike SLBMs, which can be launched at near-intercontinental distances, the shorter-range SLCMs might require that submarines or surface ships travel farther to reach their launch points. While in transit, those carriers could be detected, thus defeating the purpose of the surprise attack. Even if the United States did not detect enemy forces, delay of the larger missile attack while waiting for precursor forces to be positioned might pose an unacceptable risk in the minds of Soviet planners.

Even if accomplished with total surprise, the precursor attack would not threaten the U.S. with decapitation. Only part of the retaliatory force and part of its supporting C³ structure could be destroyed, as explained further below. Instead, as Ted Postol says, the threat of a small surprise attack is merely a "nuisance" to planners and a potential impediment to the smooth working of the U.S. deterrent.[6] It is a nuisance, however, that could not be ignored by a conservative planner. Postol believes that "U.S. strategic planners *will* take the leading edge attack seriously, *will* spend money to defeat it, and *will* adjust assessment of the adequacy of the U.S. strategic posture to take it into account." Fear of a debilitating precursor attack obviously decreases crisis stability by making preemption appear more attractive. In addition, the prospect of an attack without warning could conceivably prompt changes in force postures or operational procedures (such as launch under attack) already stressed by the short warning times of ballistic missiles.

Precursor Threat to Bombers and Command Aircraft.
The vulnerability of aircraft decreases rapidly once they become airborne. Furthermore, unlike ICBMs and SLBMs, bombers can be ordered aloft and recalled if necessary. Several provisions allow the approximately one-third of the strategic bomber force that is routinely kept on 15-minute runway alert to be sent aloft in an emergency without relinquishment of control over the release of nuclear weapons by higher authority.

In a positive control launch (PCL), bombers are ordered not to fly beyond predesignated holding points outside enemy territory. Although a positive control launch is a provocative act, it is not irrevocable and would not, by itself, lead to nuclear release. In order to arm a bomber-carried nuclear weapon, an Emergency Action Message from the NCA must be received to deactivate electronic locks (permissive action links, PALs). This fact, along with the vulnerability of the force before takeoff, explains why PCL authority for bombers and PACCS aircraft is not reserved exclusively for the presidential command level but is delegated to the Commander-in-Chief of the Strategic Air Command (CINCSAC). A PCL could be ordered by CINC-SAC or his alternate; preparatory actions such as ordering crewmen into their planes, starting engines, and taxiing would not even require an authority this high.[7] (However, the vulnerability of bombers on the ground while being recycled after a positive launch would add to the reluctance of military leaders to consider PCL without unambiguous warning.) Authority to launch alternate airborne command posts and communication relays is dispersed among the other CINCs who control nuclear weapons. An enemy attempting to prevent PCL launch would thus have to contend with these subordinate commands in addition to SAC's continuously airborne command post, "Looking Glass," and the recently authorized mobile command posts. Both of the latter are presently untargetable.

Bombers might also be attacked directly by a precursor attack. Only a fraction of SAC's bombers and tankers are routinely based near the coast. In a crisis, these aircraft could be dispersed to inland bases. If, despite the high risk the attacker would face, one fears that even bombers and airborne command posts based in the interior of the United States are vulnerable to direct cruise missile or bomber attack, then added surveillance barriers located inside the United States or point surveillance around air bases would be necessary. The minimal surveillance goal would be to provide the same 15 minutes of unambiguous warning that planners assume they would have in an SLBM attack; this would call for detecting subsonic cruise missiles roughly 100– 125 miles out.

While detailing a specific architecture for defending SAC bases is beyond the scope of this paper, one could imagine surrounding SAC bases by a ring of forward-based, short-range ground radars to detect low-altitude bombers and cruise missiles, and placing one or more long-range radars near the base to detect high-altitude aircraft. Acoustic detectors and ground-based radars might also be used synergistically to detect low-flying air vehicles. Tethered balloons or airships (blimps) could be adapted for continuous airborne surveillance, since their vulnerability to attack does not diminish their usefulness for warning. AWACS on alert or helicopter-mounted radar are more survivable alternatives.

Balloons and airships cannot fly as high as aircraft, but even at an altitude of 7500 feet the radar horizon is approximately 125 miles—just far enough to give a warning horizon of about 15 minutes for subsonic bombers and cruise missiles. The identification problem that is so vexing in peacetime could be considerably simplified in a crisis by grounding private and commercial air traffic. However, the grounding of aircraft would only be practical in a grave crisis and it would be difficult to sustain for more than a few days.

Precursor Attacks on Missile Warning Sensors. Instead of targeting the bomber force directly, a precursor attack might seek to disrupt early warning missile sensors so that a follow-on SLBM or ICBM strike could not be detected or assessed. Disruption of sensors or their communication links to national command centers, even if accomplished covertly, would still provide a type of warning. How the loss of sensor data would be interpreted and what actions might follow would depend on such factors as whether sensor outage occurred during an ongoing conventional or nuclear crisis, whether sensor outage happened routinely, and the existence and reliability of corroborating data.

In a crisis or if strategic warning were available, American leaders might regard sensor outage as conclusive evidence that an attack was occurring. Sensor outage due to nuclear attack might be accompanied by other evidence of an attack in progress. For example, space-based nuclear burst detectors (the Nuclear Detonation System, NDS) are being placed on satellites in the Navstar Global Positioning Satellite (GPS) constellation. With redundant communication links to ground and airborne command posts, NDS is meant to provide attack assessment and verification of nuclear detonation to NCA in both a pre- and post-attack period.[8] In addition to NDS, other nuclear burst (electro-magnetic pulse, EMP) detectors, which could be covert (ground-based) or untargetable (mounted on aircraft), could provide decision-makers with additional evidence that an attack was in progress.[9] Attacks on sensors could conceivably even trigger a U.S. decision to execute a launch-under-attack (LUA) option.

Missile warning sensors are both ground- and space-based. A precursor attack on ground-based missile warning radar, by a conventional or nuclear weapon carried by an aircraft or cruise missile, would still leave infrared early warning sensors in geosynchronous orbit available to detect SLBM or ICBM attacks on bomber bases. Attacks on satellite ground receiving and process-ing stations are possible; however, some ground stations are being made mobile as part of a continuing C^3 upgrade.

If an attack on sensors were accompanied by an attack on the NCA, data from surviving sensors might be irrelevant. However, in scenarios other than a bolt from the blue, other parts of the command structure might have been alerted and provisions for rapid transfer of authority to release nuclear weapons under the SIOP (Single Integrated Operational Plan, the U.S. nuclear war plan) might be in place. Furthermore, while there is some potential for spoofing early warning sensors, the destruction of Washington, D.C., by a nuclear weapon would not go unnoticed by surviving military commands. The destruction of Washington and the NCA would not prevent CINCSAC, his alternate, or Looking Glass from ordering aloft the bombers, tank-ers, and airborne command posts. Orders to flush these aircraft could travel through surviving portions of the communication network, or be relayed through the ground-wave emergency network (GWEN), a network of EMP-hardened low-frequency radio relays that is currently being deployed.

Preventing a Soviet "Free Ride"

The mission referred to as "preventing a Soviet free ride" seeks to increase Soviet defense expenditures and reduce the weight of a Soviet bomber attack by forcing Soviet leaders to continually upgrade their air-breathing forces and to plan on using only their most capable bombers in war. While many analysts speak of the importance of this mission, it is difficult to specify the type of defense it entails.

Air defenses could force Soviet leaders to procure only capable and expensive strategic bombers for wartime use, if Soviet planners fear that less sophisticated penetrating bombers would face an unacceptable risk of detection or destruction en route to target. A bomber might, for example, have an unacceptably large radar cross section, or insufficient range to fly low-altitude penetration paths to avoid radar detection and reduce vulnerability to air defense weapons.[10] The high cost of procuring modern strategic bombers imposes practical limits on force size. Unit costs for development and production of the latest U.S. penetrating bombers, the B-1B and the B-2, are approximately $280 and some $575 million (assuming a production run of 132), respectively.

In addition to reducing the number of aircraft that would participate in an attack, nuclear payloads of each bomber might also decrease as gravity bombs are replaced with fewer numbers of heavier stand-off weapons (cruise missiles and short-range attack missiles), and as the vehicle is loaded with defensive avionics. An extreme view of air defense's role in preventing a free ride even envisions the Soviets' abandonment of plans for modernization in the face of robust U.S. defense. However, while air defenses may have some impact on the weapons acquisition process, their effect appears to be limited to shifting the emphasis among modernization choices.

A legitimate question is whether continental air defenses can have much impact on Soviet bomber procurement and employment strategy in the absence of a ballistic missile defense to protect vulnerable air defense resources. With the exception of AWACS and fighter-interceptors, U.S. air defense is highly vulnerable to ground attack. AWACS and fighter-interceptors are in turn dependent on tactical warning for survival, limited in endurance (even with airborne refueling, they could not stay up more than a day or so), and dependent on vulnerable ground dispersal bases for maintenance and refueling.

Despite the vulnerability of U.S. air defenses, some analysts assert that conservative Soviet planners will invariably make a worst case analysis and attribute more capability to U.S. defenses than U.S. planners do. According to this argument, the United States can reap some of the benefits of air defense with only minimal investment. In fact, a minimal air defense was maintained by the United States during the 1960s and 1970s partly for these reasons. While critics believe it is an unnecessary extravagance now, government and Air Force officials view the current modernization program as a prudent investment in maintaining this policy.

Defense against Terrorist or Small Country Attack

The preoccupation of some U.S. officials with the possibility of a Soviet accidental ballistic missile launch or a deliberate terrorist attack suggests the potential for a corresponding mission for air defense. An airplane would appear to be at least as likely a weapon for a terrorist as a ballistic missile, given the relative ease of procurement.

Defense against terrorist air attack poses operational and technical challenges unlikely to be met during peacetime for even the most robust air defense system. All targets would have to be detected, identified, intercepted, and, if hostile, destroyed before they penetrated the 21,000-km perimeter of North America or the 14,000-km border of the continental United States.

NORAD includes "raid recognition" as one of its missions. But attempting to characterize a single uncorrelated radar track amid peacetime air traffic would require new detection algorithms that would inevitably raise the false alarm rate. For example, small aircraft taking off from locations in the United States and flying under commercial air corridors are not required to file flight plans. Until recently, NORAD did not even track aircraft flying at speeds under 180 knots, because no military aircraft fly this slowly. (The recent change is to aid drug interception efforts.)

Monitoring the borders against terrorist attack is at least as difficult as controlling the flow of contraband into the United States via aircraft. In response to Congressional pressure for the military to assume a more active role in drug enforcement, an Air Force official estimated that 110 AWACS aircraft would be needed to seal off U.S. borders against drug traffic.[11] The Air Force now has 34 AWACS aircraft. Acquiring 76 new AWACS would cost over $15 billion, apart from the cost of new bases and operation and support.

Under U.S. and Canadian peacetime rules of engagement, all unidentified targets require visual identification before hostile actions are taken. In fact, an international agreement signed by the United States forbids the use of any force, even warning shots, to intercept civil aircraft. An unidentified aircraft detected off the coast of North America that was suspected of being on a terrorist raid would have to be intercepted in international airspace. Interceptors on 5-minute alert might be able to travel 600 miles with one hour of warning, the most that might be expected. Bases would thus have to be spaced approximately 1000 miles apart all around the border. Current air defense interceptors, while potent fighters, might have difficulty if vectored to intercept slow-flying aircraft. A Pentagon spokesman commenting on the possibility of using military aircraft to interdict drug smugglers noted that an F-16 (whose minimum speed is faster than the typical speed of a small propeller-driven aircraft) would be unable to intercept a slow-flying aircraft without shooting it down.[12]

A terrorist could also be expected to disguise the intent of his mission; conceivably an attack could even be staged from a commercial airliner with landing rights in the United States. Finally, even if surveillance sensors and detection algorithms were capable of detecting a terrorist attack, and even if the United States were prepared to acquire interceptors in sufficient numbers and at sufficient locations to perform the IFF (identification friend-or-foe) mission, the more likely avenues for terrorist attack—for example, weapons smuggled in overland from Canada or Mexico or by ship along the long U.S. coastline—would still remain and would become increasingly likely to be used as the air defense system was buttressed.

Deterrence is based on a credible threat of retaliation. Discounting the "madman" scenario which by definition cannot be deterred, an attack by a nation that possesses a small air force that could reach CONUS is already deterred. Nevertheless, if the capability to defeat such an attack is desired, then the same difficulties discussed above apply.

Defense of Selected Deterrent Forces

The point defense mission seeks to provide local defense of retaliatory forces and selected command and communication targets from air-breathing attack. It is assumed that a ballistic missile defense (BMD) is deployed along with an air defense, and that a large ballistic missile attack would precede air attack. The strategic forces at risk would be ICBMs not launched or destroyed, bombers not launched or destroyed (many of these will be the non-alert portion of the bomber force), and submarines in port. Also at risk are associated command centers, warning sensors, and communication links that would tie these forces to the NCA.

Point air defenses would be located in the vicinity of ICBMs, SAC bases, and targets not collocated with large population centers. These targets could be protected by only the terminal stages of a layered ballistic missile defense.[13] For an enduring defense, air defense would have to protect the BMD components and vice versa. Since the destination of air attackers is assumed to be known, SAMs remain the most economical choice for local air defense.

The United States is considering road-mobile and rail-mobile ICBMs to reduce the vulnerability of land-based missiles to a Soviet first strike.[14] However, even mobile ICBMs could be vulnerable to a follow-on air attack by manned aircraft. Robert Everett, until recently the chairman of the Defense Science Board, points out that "mobile missiles, especially in desert areas, may be vulnerable to bomber attack and may survive only a few hours under attack unless provided with very costly air defenses."[15]

The key question for targeting mobile, relocatable, or reconstitutable forces that survive a ballistic missile attack is whether near-real-time intelligence would be available after a nuclear exchange to guide follow-on missile or air attackers to their targets. To date, there are no proven solutions to this problem.[16]

It is not known whether Soviet doctrine calls for attacking mobile and relocatable targets in the United States. Holding Soviet mobile and relocatable targets at risk *is* a high priority for the U.S. Air Force.[17] The U.S. Air Force is committed to using the manned penetrating bomber for this mission, and justifies the development of the Stealth bomber partly on the premise that surviving Soviet air defenses could not stop it from reaching its target.

Should the United States decide that an air defense is necessary for its mobile missiles, the obvious choice would be a mobile SAM system. Some SAMs are already mobile, and even relatively large systems could be adapted to special trucks or road vehicles. Fixed SAMs are also possible in an architecture where point missile and air defenses are deployed together on a military reservation, and mobile missiles dash between protected sites.

In addition to the possibility of destroying enemy aircraft directly, the existence of SAM systems in mobile ICBM deployment regions might force enemy aircraft to fly low, thereby increasing their fuel consumption. Low altitude flight might also increase aircraft vulnerability to dust ingestion and other effects from nearby explosions. Perhaps the most important effect of low altitude flight would be to reduce the line-of-sight range of on-board visible, infrared, and radar sensors searching for mobile targets.

Damage Limitation through Nationwide Defense

Damage limitation is the most ambitious of the active defense missions. SDI architectures for nationwide defense assume a layered defense. In the first, outer-most defensive layer, space-based defenses attack ascending ballistic missiles in their boost phase before they release reentry vehicles, decoys, or penetration aids. Corresponding air defense architectures envision an analogous outer-layer defense extending east-west across the Canadian Arctic and some 2000 miles offshore. The primary goal of the outer-layer defense would be to shoot down cruise missile carriers before they reached their launch points. A surveillance barrier at least several hundred miles deep would be necessary to provide sufficient time for the defense to employ shoot-look-shoot tactics to increase their probability of kill. The outer-layer defense would also attempt to destroy ALCMs and SLCMs launched from the innermost portion of the surveillance barrier.

The surveillance and weapon systems for this mission are only in a concept stage. Among the most frequently mentioned outer-layer surveillance systems are space-based radars (SBRs) or a chain of high-altitude remotely piloted vehicles (RPVs), each carrying a radar transmitter and receiver. Hybrid systems have also been proposed in which the RPVs carry a receiver for signals transmitted from SBRs.

Engagement of aircraft and cruise missiles thousands of miles from U.S. borders is not possible with interceptors based on the U.S. mainland. Forward basing of interceptors and airborne early warning aircraft on naval carrier task forces is one way to project airpower to distant locations, but is also extremely expensive. The ideal weapon for outer-layer engagement would be a very long range SAM, but this weapon is still in an early stage of development and would have to overcome many technical challenges to become practical and cost-effective.

Aircraft that leak through the outer-layer defense would be engaged by a second defensive layer consisting of AWACS or AWACS variants and manned fighter interceptors or long-range missiles. Alternatively, an armed transport that combined surveillance radars and a large number of long-range air-to-air missiles in a large airframe might be employed. The middle layer must also engage ALCMs and SLCMs. The SLCM threat could be eased somewhat by a naval ASW effort in the seas near the coast. By forcing SLCM-carrying ships and submarines further offshore, the defense would acquire valuable battlespace. In addition, underwater detection might be easier away from shallow coastal waters.

Terminal air defenses in the third layer might be based on short-range SAM systems. Alternatively, AWACS or helicopter-based radar could take off on tactical warning and provide guidance updates to long-range SAMs launched from a small number of locations within the United States. By concentrating SAMs at limited locations, the defense has a better chance of defeating saturation attacks that attempt to overwhelm local defenses along a particular attack corridor. But concentrating the SAMs at a handful of sites increases their vulnerability to ballistic missile attack.

A notional layered air defense, developed by William Delaney of Lincoln Laboratory for purposes of discussion at the CSIA-CIIPS air defense conference, would defend the twenty largest U.S. cities and fifty military targets from an attack by 3000 cruise missiles (1000 SLCMs and 2000 ALCMs). It would also be designed to provide substantial area defense to Canada, Alaska, and Hawaii. The defensive goal would be to achieve a leakage rate of one in a thousand. Since, historically, complex SAM systems achieve at best a single-shot kill probability of 0.5–0.7, the defense would need 6–10 independent kill opportunities in order to achieve leakage rates of 0.001. Table 2-1 shows the cost of Delaney's notional defense.

These estimates do not include the cost of BMD

TABLE 2-1. COST ESTIMATES FOR NOTIONAL
DEFENSE OF NORTH AMERICA.

Component	Number Needed	Unit Cost	Total Cost
Space Radar	8–20	$750 M–1 B	$ 6–20 B
Advanced Air-borne Surveillance Track Systems	40–50	200–400 M	8–20 B
Long-range Missiles	5,000–10,000	5–10 M	25–100 B
SAM Batteries	200–300	75–100 M	15–30 B
TOTAL			$54–170 B

SOURCE: W.P. Delaney, "Air Defense of the United States: A View of Strategic Air Defense Missions and Modern Air Defense Technology," Project Report CMT-141 (Lexington, Mass.: MIT Lincoln Laboratory, May 10, 1989), Table 5-2. Reprinted with permission, Lincoln Laboratory, MIT, Lexington, Mass.

components needed to protect air defense bases and SAM sites, lifetime operational and support costs, manning costs, or ASW costs. This defense utilizes systems still in the early stages of development, and it does not take into account adversary responsiveness. Delaney's notional defense is not unique, but other permutations reveal the same lesson: heavy air defenses based on near-term technology would be extraordinarily expensive.[18]

Air Defense and Ballistic Missile Defense: Parallels and Distinctions

The rationale and technical feasibility of BMD have been thoroughly explored by the policy-making and technical community on at least three occasions—at the beginning and at the end of the 1960s, and more recently in connection with SDI. This chapter on air defense missions will conclude by comparing and contrasting BMD and air defense with respect to: 1) their overlap with other military missions; 2) prospects for arms control; and 3) the problems of identification in peacetime. The objective is to highlight some differences between what might otherwise appear to be analogous activities.

Overlap with Other Missions. As long as it abides by the ABM treaty, the United States cannot deploy BMD except at agreed sites in militarily insignificant numbers. Barring unforeseen advances in SDI, the United States will continue for at least the near future to have reliable and timely warning of ballistic missile launches, but no possibility of defense against them.

In contrast, air defenses are already ubiquitous. They are found in the defensive forces of most nations and have roles such as air traffic control that have no parallel with BMD. Although the United States let its strategic air defenses atrophy after the 1950s, theater air defense continued to be modernized and supported, especially in NATO. The weapons, surveillance systems, and command and control for theater defense overlap those appropriate for continental defense. (The largest visible difference now is not in the technology, but in deployments: by the end of the 1970s all SAMs had been removed from CONUS.) This overlap means that an arms control regime that sought to impose militarily significant limits on strategic air defense would probably not be possible without impinging on what are considered vital conventional military missions.

Arms Control. Does the difficulty of establishing an arms control regime for air defense preclude agreements on limits for offensive air-breathing forces? Interestingly, in the past, restrictions on air defense have not been considered necessary to agreements limiting air offense. In SALT II, for example, the United States allowed low limits on the air-breathing leg of its triad without restraints on Soviet air defense activities. More recently, U.S. proposals in START (the Strategic Arms Reduction Talks) seem to invite the buildup of Soviet bombers and SLCMs despite the acknowledged asymmetry in U.S. and Soviet air defense capabilities.

The effect of air defense in the START negotiations has been seen only indirectly, as the United States and the Soviet Union have agreed that strategic bombers with a penetrating role should count as only one warhead regardless of their loadings of gravity bombs and short-range attack missiles. The U.S. contention was that this counting rule was necessary to account for the effect of Soviet air defenses—presumably the United States believes that Soviet air defense might exact a price in U.S. short-range attack missiles (SRAMs) expended in defense penetration or in bombers lost en route to their targets. However, other factors appear more important than any fears the United States has of Soviet air defenses, including the difficulty of verifying internal bomber loadings, the desire to continue bomber modernization programs unimpeded by warhead ceilings, and a continuation of the Reagan policy to move from "fast-flyers" to "slow-flyers" in the belief that bombers are second-strike weapons and therefore more stabilizing.

The SALT and START negotiations suggest that air defense can be decoupled from strategic forces in arms control negotiations.[19] The ability to decouple the two is due to the perception that air defense is relatively unimportant militarily at current levels of forces, or even after potential "50 percent" cuts. However, an air defense perceived as ineffective because of its vulnerability to large numbers of weapons or to suppression by ballistic missiles might begin to seem more capable under an arms control regime that eliminated or drastically reduced ballistic missiles. If assured penetration is required for stability, a limit on ballistic missile cuts may be imposed by the effectiveness of air defenses. Complicating the picture further is the asymmetry between U.S. and Soviet air defense capabilities, which will remain even after current modernization.

Peacetime Identification. Central to "new" ideas for BMD is the possibility of attacking missiles in their boost phase using either space-based weapons or ground-based high-energy lasers with space-based relay mirrors. At first glance, boost-phase BMD might seem much more difficult than air defense. A typical speed for an ICBM third stage at burnout is 6.5 km per second—more than 25 times faster than the typical cruising speed of a long-range bomber. To intercept an ICBM in its boost phase with a space-based battle station, the defense has to acquire and track the target, compute a fire-control solution, direct a weapon along the calculated path, and confirm a kill, or shoot again. This process must be repeated for all ICBMs within range of each battle station. However, booster burnout occurs only 3–5 minutes after launch (even less if fast-burn boosters are developed); the brevity of this period of vulnerability greatly complicates these tasks. Once booster burnout occurs, target detection and tracking become substantially more difficult problems. In addition, the number of targets can increase dramatically (to perhaps thousands) if warhead decoys are dispensed from the post-boost vehicle.

In contrast, aircraft are vulnerable for hours. It is, of course, target acquisition that makes air defense such a difficult problem. The focus here is on a critical aspect of target acquisition unique to air-breathers: the IFF problem, identifying and distinguishing "friend from foe."

A missile's signature is unique; no natural phenomenon mimics the missile's combination of high speed, large infrared emission, and high trajectory. The hot plume of a rocket booster is visible to short-wave infrared detectors on satellites in geosynchronous orbits in space after the rocket rises above the lower atmosphere. The missile's post-boost vehicle, fuel tanks, and reentry vehicles, traveling on high arching trajectories, can be detected at long ranges, first by the forward-based BMEWS system of ground radars in Clear, Alaska, in Thule, Greenland, and in Fylingdales, U.K., and later by the PARCS (Perimeter Acquisition Radar Control System) phased array radar in North Dakota (the only operational remnant of the U.S. ABM system). Submarine-launched missiles are detectable with the same infrared sensors in orbit and with PAVE PAWS ground radars that face outward with overlapping coverage from four locations on the periphery of the United States.

In contrast, aircraft are not easily identified as "foes." The sky is normally filled in all directions with private, commercial and military aircraft. Unknown tracks appear on atmosphere surveillance radars at a much higher frequency than is the case for missile warning radar. If the sensitivity of atmospheric early warning systems improves, background noise from birds, friendly aircraft that have not filed flight plans, and other spurious effects will increase the false alarm rate. The seemingly mundane problem of identification may be the weak link in improved surveillance. Until this problem is solved, some of the best technical innovations for air defense may literally be "lost in the noise."

Notes

1. Tactical warning is warning of an attack in progress. For example, infrared sensors and ground-based radars can detect the launch and flight of ballistic missiles. Strategic warning is warning based on evidence collected prior to an attack. Strategic warning might come from human or sensor detection of such activities as unusual communication patterns, movement of aircraft to forward staging areas, dispersal of vulnerable forces, surging submarines from port, or interception of messages from commanders to field

units. The distinction between strategic and tactical warning becomes less clear in the period immediately preceding commencement of hostilities.

2. See Seymour M. Hersh, *The Target Is Destroyed* (New York: Random House, 1986). The KAL 007 shoot-down was a tragic illustration of the problem of visual IFF (identification friend-or-foe). The downing of an Iranian airliner on July 3, 1988, by a rocket from the *USS Vincennes* illustrated the problem of performing IFF even with state-of-the-art radar. The *Vincennes* apparently believed it was under attack from an F-14 fighter. Afterwards, the question was repeatedly asked: how could such a sophisticated radar fail to distinguish an F-14 fighter from a commercial Airbus? In fact, such a distinction is difficult because the size of a radar return is a function of range, viewing angle, target composition and shape, etc. Moreover, it is not clear that the radar on U.S. warships (or on SAM systems) even attempts to do IFF based on radar return because of the obvious possibility of enemy spoofing. In any case, the software that processed the raw radar data for display on the radar screens of the *Vincennes* reportedly did not display the magnitude of the radar return. See Russell Watson, "A Case of Human Error," *Newsweek*, August 15, 1988, p. 20.

3. The National Command Authority consists of the president and the secretary of defense, or their duly constituted successors. Only the NCA can authorize the use of nuclear weapons.

4. The elements of the command and communications network that are continuously airborne are least vulnerable to surprise attack. These include the Looking Glass command post of SAC and two Navy TACAMO VLF (very low frequency) communication relays over the Atlantic and Pacific oceans. Upon tactical warning, other parts of the PACCS (post-attack command and control aircraft) fleet will be launched. Among them are the national emergency airborne command post (NEACP, or "kneecap"), a platform for the NCA; two alternate airborne command posts; three airborne missile launch control centers; and two airborne communication relays. In addition, parts of the World Wide Airborne Nuclear Command Posts (WWANCP) are expected to take off. These include the airborne command posts of the Atlantic and Pacific "nuclear CINCS" (commanders-in-chief of unified commands who oversee nuclear forces, CINCLANT and CINCPAC), stationed off the Atlantic coast and in Hawaii. CINCEUR, stationed in England, and backup TACAMOs would probably also take off.

5. There would be extra time, if strategic warning were available, or if an attack occurred during an ongoing crisis. The extra time could be used to mobilize forces, prepare for the orderly transfer of command, and undertake other survivability measures. Examples of these actions include: flushing MX from garrison (if plans for rail-based mobile MX basing are carried out), alerting theater military commands, moving non-alert forces to a higher state of readiness, dispersing ground-mobile command and communication backups, dispersing on the ground or sending aloft non-alert air defense interceptors and AWACS, and surging nuclear ballistic missile submarines (SSBNs) and nuclear attack submarines (SSNs) from port. In an extreme emergency it is even possible that SAC could reinstate an airborne alert for part of its bomber force, a practice discontinued in 1968. Finally, if attack appeared imminent, the president, or more likely the vice president, could take off in the National Emergency Airborne Command Post.

6. Theodore A. Postol, "Banning Nuclear SLCMs: It Would Be Nice If We Could," *International Security*, Vol. 13, No. 3 (Winter 1988/89), pp. 191–202. For a discussion of the prospects for a decapitation attack, see Ashton B. Carter, "Assessing Command System Vulnerability," in Ashton B. Carter, John D. Steinbruner, and Charles Zraket, eds., *Managing Nuclear Operations* (Washington, D.C.: Brookings, 1987).

7. On two occasions in June 1980, when indications of an SLBM attack erroneously appeared at the SAC command post, the SAC duty controller directed all alert crews to move to their aircraft and start engines in preparation for takeoff. During one of the incidents, following established procedure, the Pacific Command airborne command post also took off. These preparatory procedures took place in peacetime with no corroborating indicators of an impending attack. "Recent False Alerts from the Nation's Missile Attack Warning System," Hearings before the Senate Committee on Armed Services, 96th Cong., 2d sess. (Washington, D.C.: U.S. GPO, 1980).

8. The NDS package provides detection and geo-location of nuclear bursts. The Navstar/Global Positioning Satellite (GPS) constellation and the NDS detector and communications package incorporate a number of survivability features. See Ashton B. Carter, "Satellites and Anti-Satellites: The Limits of the Possible," *International Security*, Vol. 10, No. 4 (Spring 1986), pp. 46–98.

9. The United States is reportedly planning to field ground-based EMP detectors as part of the AACE (Aircraft Alerting Com-

munications EMP protection system). The detectors are supposed to alert airbase commanders that an EMP event has occurred and that emergency communication systems should be used. John Haystead, "AF C³ Procurement Centers," *Journal of Electronic Defense*, April 1986, p. 34.

10. Aerodynamic drag forces are proportional to the density of air (greatest near the earth's surface) and the square of the relative wind velocity of the aircraft. Forcing an aircraft to fly at low altitudes thus creates greater drag and increases fuel consumption. The penalty for low altitude flight is especially severe for aircraft originally designed for high altitude penetration, such as the B-52. In contrast, the U.S. B-1B and Soviet Blackjack were designed from the start to fly for extended periods at low altitude. For data on B-1B range as a function of payload and flight profile, see U.S. Congress, Congressional Budget Office, *The B-1B Bomber and Options for Enhancements* (Washington, D.C.: U.S. GPO, August 1988).

11. Paul Mann, "Congress Pressures Military to Assume Direct Antidrug Role," *Aviation Week and Space Technology*, May 23, 1988, p. 25. These numbers could, of course, be reduced if intelligence were available to indicate the likely target for a terrorist attack.

12. Pentagon spokesman Dan Howard on *CBS Evening News*, May 12, 1988.

13. SDI research has focused on the use of conventional ground-based chemical rockets (SAM systems) for the terminal layer. Designers are studying two systems, one for exo-atmospheric intercept (ERIS) and one for endo-atmospheric intercept (HEDI). Concepts for ground-based terminal BMD appear far more feasible in the near term than space-based defense. For example, see Chapter 5 in Office of Technology Assessment (OTA), *SDI: Technology, Survivability, and Software*, Report OTA-ISC-353 (Washington, D.C.: U.S. GPO, May 1988).

14. See Barry E. Fridling and John R. Harvey, "On the Wrong Track? An Assessment of MX Rail Garrison Basing," *International Security*, Vol. 13, No. 3 (Winter 1988/89), pp. 113–141.

15. Robert R. Everett, "Forget the Midgetman; Build MXs," *Technology Review*, November–December 1986, p. 28.

16. The target acquisition problem is central to the feasibility of targeting mobile and other strategic relocatable targets. Although systems for monitoring troop movements, tanks, artillery, etc., from airborne platforms are being developed, they would have limited capabilities for real-time surveillance of the nuclear battlefield. Sen-

sor systems based on radar, visible, or infrared detection would have to operate in the presence of background radiation, dust, and fire. Long-range communications would be essential to provide ICBMs, SLBMs, or distant aircraft with the locations of mobile targets. However, over-the-horizon radio links that use HF frequencies are expected to be disrupted for hours or even days after nuclear detonations, and in a wartime environment, space-based surveillance and communication satellites might be attacked directly or their ground terminals might be destroyed.

17. General John T. Chain, Jr., CINCSAC, testimony before the Senate Armed Services Committee (SASC), July 21, 1989, Senate Hearing 101–332, "Testing and Operational Requirements for the B-2 Bomber," pp. 8–20. See also Desmond Ball and Robert C. Toth, "Revising the SIOP: Taking War-fighting to Dangerous Extremes," *International Security*, Vol. 14, No. 4 (Spring 1990), pp. 65–92.

18. Barry Blechman and Victor Utgoff have presented a notional air defense that uses available technology with somewhat improved performance that would complement a comprehensive BMD and be leakproof against the projected Soviet cruise missile threat of the 1990s. Blechman and Utgoff, "The Macroeconomics of Strategic Defenses," *International Security*, Vol. 11, No. 3 (Winter 1986/87), pp. 33–70.

19. Herbert York cites SALT II to support his argument that strategic defense is not intrinsically incompatible with arms control. York, *Does Strategic Defense Breed Offense?* CSIA Occasional Paper No. 1 (Lanham, Md.: University Press of America, 1987), p. 27.

Chapter 3

RADAR DETECTION, EVASION AND THE STEALTH CHALLENGE

In the 1990s the threat from stealth aircraft and cruise missiles will be the dominant factor in U.S. strategic air defense planning. Low-observable cruise missiles are a particular concern. As the United States and USSR begin to deploy thousands of dual-capable (that is, conventional and nuclear) cruise missiles on strategic aircraft, surface ships, and submarines, there is the unsettling prospect of a future in which weapons are easily proliferated, nuclear and conventional types are indistinguishable, and assured warning is uncertain.

While the course of debate on air defense will be determined as much by political as technical concerns, knowledge of the basic technologies is necessary for understanding the issues. As background for the discussion of air defense technologies, this chapter reviews some fundamentals of radar detection and evasion, and outlines new challenges posed by stealth and the possibilities for detection by radar.

Radar Cross Section

Radar is the most important technology for air defense. It is the only detection method capable of long-range,

53

all-weather, day and night operation, and it is a key element in virtually all surveillance and weapons systems.

The signal returned from an object to a radar is a function of the incident power on the target and the radar reflectivity of the target. The power that illuminates the target is determined by the transmitted power, the transmitting antenna size (a larger antenna allows the power to be concentrated into a narrower beam), the distance from transmitter to target, and atmospheric attenuation. How much of the reflected energy is captured by a radar receiver depends on its distance from the receiver, atmospheric attenuation, and the receiving antenna size. Not all of the signal returned to the radar receiver is due to reflections from the target. Background "noise" is inevitable from natural phenomena and from spurious radar returns, including ground radar returns if some of the beam intercepts the earth. Some noise is also added to the signal by the radar's electronics.

The radar reflectivity of a target is usually expressed in terms of "radar cross section" (RCS)—a measure of the reflection area of a target in the direction of the radar receiver. The RCS is defined as the area of a fictitious perfect reflector of electromagnetic waves that would reflect the same amount of energy back to the radar as the actual target does.

Radar cross sections are difficult to calculate from first principles. They are a sensitive function of an object's shape, its construction materials, the radar-target geometry (including polarization effects), and the radar frequency. An object that is an efficient radar scatterer at one wavelength may be poor at another. Targets whose surface texture is smooth compared to the wavelength of the illuminating signal can act like a mirror and produce much larger radar echoes than physically larger curved surfaces, assuming the radar-target geometry is favorable.[1] Table 3-1 shows typical head-on radar cross sections at microwave frequencies.[2]

A large portion of the radar return from an aircraft viewed head-on comes from the front of the engine. The control fins and sharp corners or other discontinuities in the body contour are other sources of large radar returns. A significant part of the B-52 bomber's large frontal radar cross section comes from its eight large turbofan engines that face forward. The B-1B bomber's engines were placed at the end of a long curved duct designed to minimize forward radar scatter.

Recent military aircraft have demonstrated that dramatic reductions in radar cross section are possible. The

TABLE 3-1. RADAR CROSS SECTIONS.

Object	RCS (m²)
Pickup truck	200
Automobile	100
Jumbo jet airliner	100
Large bomber or commercial jet	40
Cabin cruiser boat	10
Large fighter aircraft	6
Small fighter aircraft or four-passenger jet	2
Cessna 172	1
Adult male human	1
Bird	0.01
Insect	0.00001

SOURCE: Except RCS of Cessna 172, added by the author, data are from John A. Adam, "How to Design an 'Invisible' Aircraft," *IEEE Spectrum*, April 1988, p. 28, based on data in Merrill I. Skolnik, *Introduction to Radar Systems* (New York: McGraw Hill, 1980).
NOTE: These figures are meant only for broad comparisons, as RCS varies greatly for a single object, depending on the illumination wavelength, aspect angle, and radar polarization.

reduction in RCS from the B-52 to the B-1B is said to be approximately a factor of 100. Because of their small size and low-altitude flight paths, cruise missiles are inherently difficult to detect with radar.[3] Published accounts of cruise missiles report cross sections of 0.1 m², at least one order of magnitude less than the B-1.[4]

One should be careful, however, in interpreting the operational significance of these reductions. Usually RCS is stated for a particular frequency, assuming radar illumination close to head-on. The reduction in radar cross section from the B-52 to the B-1B is presumably less dramatic if the radar illumination is nearly overhead or from below, where large wing surfaces are nearly perpendicular to the beam. While ground search radars view distant targets nearly head-on, over-the-horizon radars view targets from above. Targets attempting to cross a surveillance line formed by higher altitude airborne radars will also expose parts of their wing surfaces.

Stealth and Its Effects

The United States is thought to lead the world in developing "stealth" technologies, an amalgam of techniques to reduce the visibility of aircraft to radar and infrared detectors. Passive stealth techniques include using radar-absorbing materials (RAM), substituting novel composite materials and plastics for more reflective metal, and modifying air vehicle shape to redirect an impinging radar signal away from its source. Active techniques are meant to alter or even cancel the radar echo by emitting additional signals. These techniques rely on advanced signal processing and fast electronics to decipher the incoming radar signal and prepare a false echo in real time.

The B-2 Stealth bomber, now being flight-tested, is expected to have a substantially lower RCS than the B-1B.[5] The unusual shape of the aircraft—essentially a flying wing with no fuselage or tail—is a dramatic example of the use of aircraft shaping to reduce radar echo. The aircraft's length is little more than that of the F-15 fighter aircraft. Wing and body surfaces are blended together to avoid sharp discontinuities, and radar-absorbing material is apparently used at places where discontinuities are unavoidable. The aircraft cockpit windows are not clear, an indication that they have been coated with radar-absorbing material. In addition to minimizing radar echo, the B-2 has also been designed to reduce engine infrared and acoustic emissions.

The B-2 solves the problem of engine radar backscatter to ground radars by placing the engines over the wings and giving the inlets a very low profile. Replacing metal structures with less reflective fiber-reinforced materials and radar absorbing carbon-fiber composites is another stealth technique reportedly incorporated on a large scale into the B-2 design. Substituting composite materials for metal also saves weight.

Some of the stealth techniques used on the B-2 are not new. In World War II, Germany developed both narrow-band and broad-band microwave absorbers to conceal submarine periscopes from emerging radar technology. The U.S. Air Force has had an active program in RCS reduction since the early 1960s. High-altitude reconnaissance aircraft dating back to the U-2, introduced in 1961, and continuing with the SR-71 Blackbird (now being retired) have used shaping and special skin coatings to reduce radar cross section.[6]

What is revolutionary about the B-2 is that, from its inception, stealth has been its highest priority, so that it traded away some desirable characteristics to achieve unprecedented reductions in radar and infrared visibility. The B-2 does not have a supersonic capability, in contrast to the swing-wing B-1B. The payload and number of weapons that can be carried on the B-2 are thought to be less than the B-1B, in part because the B-2 must carry all its weapons in internal bays to reduce radar backscatter (as well as to improve aerodynamics). In addition, the weight of radar-absorbing material and its effect on performance may be significant. Historically, the necessity to protect delicate RAM structures is reflected in the Air Force announcement that it will build 120 "maintenance docks" (small hangars), at a cost of approximately $2 billion, to protect every B-2 bomber, including those on runway alert, from environmental effects such as the sun's ultraviolet radiation. The docks will also prevent the exposure of the B-2 to freezing rain, thus avoiding the necessity to use de-icing sprays. The dock will be air-conditioned, because the B-2 cockpit cannot be opened.[7] Most of all, the B-2 traded off economy for stealth. A current estimate of the total cost for 132 aircraft is about $75 billion, or about $575 million for each aircraft. Some analysts believe even these figures understate the true costs. Unit costs will certainly be higher if, as now seems likely, the full fleet of 132 aircraft is not produced.

What advantages are gained for these high costs? Stealth reduces radar range and the time a target is under radar coverage, and increases the defense's vulnerability to electronic countermeasures, decoys, and spoofing. In an engagement between air defense and a penetrator, these factors can combine synergistically to give the offense a marked advantage. Proponents of the stealth bomber also argue that stealth might allow bombers to fly at high altitudes even in the presence of ground air defenses, a very important advantage for searching out mobile targets, and that stealth could spur the Soviets to make extremely costly improvements in air defense.[8] They further argue that the costs of a penetrating bomber should be measured by the low cost per deliverable warhead, not the high cost per aircraft.[9] Perhaps the best argument for stealth aircraft has been made by Jasper Welch, whose analysis takes account of the impact of stealth on theater conflicts.[10]

Reduced radar range translates into somewhat reduced time under radar coverage for stealthy aircraft seeking to elude a surveillance system, a fire control radar, or an air-to-air or surface-to-air radar homing missile. The fact that range increases only gradually as RCS increases might be reassuring to the defense, were it not that RCS reductions have been quite dramatic, for example, by a factor of 100 from the B-52 to the B-1B, and a factor of 1,000 or more from the B-52 to the cruise missile. Reductions in RCS by factors of 10, 100, 1,000, and 10,000 translate into reductions in range by factors of at least 1.8, 3.2, 5.6, and 10, respectively.

Reduced RCS could have especially important consequences for engagements with airborne radars. Airborne-mounted radars like AWACS have a circular "dead zone" below the aircraft where target detection is precluded. It is conceivable that a stealth cruise missile might have a maximum detection range smaller than the radius of the dead zone, making the missile effectively invisible to AWACS. Even a somewhat more easily detected cruise missile would allow only a few minutes of radar coverage.[11]

The effect of stealth is also pronounced in the contest between electronic countermeasures (ECM) and electronic counter-countermeasures (ECCM). Searching for small targets increases vulnerability to jamming and allows the offense greater ability to use both real and electronic decoys. A B-52 attempting to spoof the defense with electronic simulation of its radar return faces a substantially different problem from a B-1B attempting a similar trick. Decoys simulating small-RCS aircraft or cruise missiles could play the same role for penetrating air-breathers that penetration aids play for ballistic missiles. The absence of an effective defense against cruise missiles has reduced the incentive to develop decoy cruise missiles until now, just as the lack of an effective ballistic missile defense has diminished the incentive to develop and deploy penetration aids.

Lowering the radar visibility of a penetrator can also stress the defense in its attempt to optimize the allocation of its weapons. Consider, for example, an engagement between an air defense consisting of fighter-interceptors with air-to-air missiles operating under the control of an AWACS, and an offense consisting of a cruise missile carrier nearing its weapons release point. In this case, the defense faces a difficult problem in assigning interceptors to targets if the cruise missile carrier is difficult to distinguish on radar from the cruise missiles themselves.

Sensitivity studies of penetrator RCS, speed, and altitude show that low RCS is the dominant factor determining time under coverage of radars that are airborne. (For ground surveillance radar or ground fire control radars, the time under radar coverage is influenced less by RCS than by the altitude and speed of the penetrator, and penetrators crossing ground radar can also make use of ground terrain to shield themselves from radar coverage.)[12]

Finally, the ability of airborne radar to detect low

altitude targets diminishes as the RCS of the target is reduced, especially over land where large and varying ground returns are inevitable. Radar countermeasures can also delay detection. The history of air engagements demonstrates that tactics, and not the traditional measures of aircraft performance such as speed, are sometimes the dominant factor in air-vehicle penetration. Stealth adds greatly to the effectiveness of the tactics the offense can employ.

High Frequency Radar

Most air defense surveillance radars, such as the airborne and ground systems referred to in the previous section, typically operate in the VHF or UHF band at frequencies from several hundred to perhaps several thousand megahertz (MHz). Radar propagation at these frequencies is limited to line-of-sight distances by the curvature of the earth. A different approach to atmospheric surveillance uses over-the-horizon propagation modes in the HF (high frequency) band at frequencies from 5 to 30 MHz.

Over-the-horizon backscatter radar (OTH-B) will be the U.S. Air Force's principal long-range atmospheric surveillance system when it is completed by the mid-1990s. OTH-B allows the surveillance of a target beyond line of sight by "bouncing" radar signals off the ionosphere. (OTH-B propagation is discussed in Chapter 4.)

OTH-B's operating frequency overlaps the resonance region for bomber-sized targets (see discussion of resonance in Chapter 4, fn. 5). Operation at the lower frequencies within the high-frequency band region generally will defeat stealth techniques based on radar-absorbing materials. At these long wavelengths, the main determinant of the RCS is the size of the aircraft, rather than smaller parts like the engine or sharp discontinuities in body shape that are responsible for radar echoes at shorter wavelengths. That is the good news for OTH-B as a stealth-defeating radar for bomber-sized targets.

But detection of smaller targets will suffer when low frequencies are used, especially at night as OTH-B moves its operating frequency towards lower frequencies in order to compensate for the reduced density of free electrons in the ionosphere. Operating at its lowest wavelength, OTH-B's radar wavelength would be some ten times larger than the length of a cruise missile, far from the ideal resonance region and well into the region where targets are very inefficient scatterers, therefore giving a very small radar echo.

OTH-B's capability to detect the current generation of cruise missiles is uncertain. Tests of OTH-B against drone aircraft simulating Soviet cruise missiles have reportedly had favorable results, but even OTH-B enthusiasts worry about the capability to detect these targets when the radar is in its normal wide-area search pattern instead of its more sensitive narrow search mode.[13] Meanwhile, designers are studying the feasibility of improving OTH-B's performance to counter an evolving cruise missile threat that incorporates stealth technology to reduce radar visibility further. One should note that simply improving the sensitivity of OTH-B will not necessarily result in improved detection capabilities if the system cannot, at a tolerable rate, discriminate real targets from false echoes. Because of its dependence on stable ionospheric conditions, a key issue for OTH-B is whether background noise from naturally occurring fluctuations in the ionosphere and other spurious effects will have the practical effect of placing a limit on OTH-B's small-target detection capability.

The next generation of U.S. cruise missile, the Advanced Cruise Missile (ACM), is nearing production. The ACM will reportedly have an increased range and a lower radar visibility than current cruise missiles. Little has been revealed about Soviet advanced cruise missile programs. What has been reported suggests that, in contrast to the United States, the Soviets are not seeking to develop a stealth cruise missile rapidly. The Soviet program to develop the SS-NX-24, a long-range, high-altitude supersonic SLCM, is consistent with this theory.

Airborne Radar

Airborne radars suffer from the practical consequences of combining in one package two dissimilar functions— long-range surveillance and tracking. They face even greater difficulty coping with low-RCS vehicles than do ground systems. Replacing current airborne radars with lower frequency radars would assist in small target detection but only at the expense of decreased resolution, increased vulnerability to jamming (a factor more important in theater air defense than strategic air defense), and greater problems with radar clutter from ground returns.[14] Because of their large weight and large size, powerful low-frequency radars are more easily adapted to ground basing than aircraft basing.

The current generation of airborne surveillance systems was designed to detect bomber-sized targets. A program to upgrade AWACS radar sensitivity by improving its signal-processing capabilities is under way, and a follow-on to AWACS, the Advanced Surveillance and Tracking System (ASTS), is a priority of the Air Defense Initiative. The goal of the ASTS program (now called Advanced Surveillance and Tracking Technologies) is to give airborne radars the same capability against cruise missiles that AWACS has against bomber-sized targets. Although the motivation for the upgrade includes strategic air defense, a larger incentive is probably the increasing reliance on airborne radar for surveillance, command and control in theater conflicts.

Beyond ASTS, contractors are busy formulating proposals for airborne radar capable of meeting an evolving low-observable threat. Very large radar antenna arrays operating at several hundred MHz (closer to cruise missile resonances than current designs) are being considered. Lockheed, for example, is experimenting with carrying large phased-array panels (45 feet long by 6 feet high) on the side of C-130 cargo transports.[15] The more distant future may see "conformal" phased arrays, in which the antenna elements are built into the skin of the aircraft. They provide a large antenna surface, and designers hope that by removing external mechanically scanned antennas, antenna support structures, and the antenna rotodome, they can produce a low-weight, minimum-drag aircraft with the potential for high altitude and long range, or long time on station.

Multistatic Radar

Radars that transmit and receive through the same antenna (monostatic radars) suffer from having to see objects from the same direction as they are illuminated. An aircraft's RCS is not only a function of frequency; it is also a sensitive function of viewing angle and is typically smaller nose-on than from other angles. For example, the stealth bomber is designed to present a very small RCS for frontal viewing, but its very large wing structure would come into view if it were illuminated with "lookdown" airborne or space-based radar, or if it flew nearly directly over a ground radar.

Bistatic radars are radars that separate the transmitter from the receiver. Aircraft that are stealthy because they have been designed to reflect radar signals away from the line-of-sight of an illuminating radar transmitter may be more visible to bistatic radars. A "multistatic" network of ground-based radars could create, for example, an electronic fence that a penetrating aircraft could not cross without being illuminated from below. Radar echoes that bounced away from the illuminating radar might still be detected by other radars in the network. Furthermore, the radar returns from the target are likely to be larger in this non-frontal viewing geometry. Multistatic radars are also more survivable than monostatic radars since the receiver can be made covert, and the system degrades gracefully if some of its components are destroyed.

Various schemes have been studied that would implement multistatic radar barriers to limit the round-trip distance between receiver and target, such as ground transmitters together with high altitude airborne reception, ground transmission and reception from a dense array of low power transmitter/receivers, and even space-based transmitters with airborne receivers. There are no obvious "winners" among these proposals; each has its own drawbacks in terms of technical risk, range, capability to locate the target sufficiently well for vectoring of interceptors, susceptibility to false alarms from birds or other objects, and cost. Nevertheless, if simple tripwire detection is acceptable and the potentially high false alarm rate can be tolerated, ground-based bistatic systems are an option for a radar barrier that would defeat stealth.

Radar "Picket Fence"

An alternative that overcomes the limitations of bistatic radars while preserving their ability to detect small RCS targets is a brute force approach which would deploy sufficient numbers of monostatic ground radars that targets could be detected nearly overhead. Ground-based microwave radars are capable of detecting small birds at a range of some 15 miles (the RCS of a bird is estimated to be .01 m²).

Deterring surprise cruise missile attacks on selected sites of high military value within the United States by creating a significant probability that they will be detected is one application for such a system. A back-of-the-envelope estimate for the cost of a surveillance system that would protect 200 sites is about $5 billion. This would buy some 400 radars similar to those being procured for the Joint Surveillance Systems. The JSS radar specifications include the capacity to detect a 0.1 m² target at 100 nautical miles.[16] (However, to be effective against low-flying targets, these radars would have to be modified to optimize their clutter rejection capabilities.) Coincidentally, 400 is also roughly the number of radars necessary to provide continuous low-altitude coverage around the entire 21,000-km perimeter of North America. Alternatively, $5 billion could purchase several thousand of the "gap-filler" type radars being used in the North Warning System for low-altitude short-range surveillance.

In summary, countering stealth is not impossible, for the stealthiest aircraft are visible at resonance frequencies, or when viewed at close range, or at angles other than head-on. The goal of creating an electronic fence that would detect the passage of a stealth target is within reach of present technology. Alternatively, a very dense network of ground line-of-sight radars might be able to deliver this detection capability, and it would also have the means to locate, identify (within the practical limits discussed above), and track incoming targets. Detection techniques based on acoustic or infrared detection are also possible, as is combining one or more detection methods with radar. However, countering stealth will be very expensive if the only solution is deploying large numbers of short-range surveillance systems. The United States is committing considerable resources to programs that aim to reduce aircraft signatures while devoting relatively little attention to programs that aim to counter stealth. This policy may prove to be short-sighted in the long run.

Notes

1. An often-cited example is a smooth, square, flat metal traffic sign. Assume the sign is a square one meter on a side. The area of the sign is one m^2, but if it is illuminated by wavelengths in the X-band, where a typical wavelength is 3 cm, its reflection would give it a radar cross section of about 14,000 m^2. This happens because, when viewed straight-on, the mirror-like reflection of the sign behaves like an antenna that is trained on the radar and reradiates all of the transmitted power it intercepts back in the radar's direction.

At X-band most of the energy is directed into a relatively narrow beam. See George W. Stimson, *Introduction to Airborne Radar* (El Segundo, Calif.: Hughes Aircraft Co., 1983), pp. 384–385, 585.

2. The designations HF (high frequency), VHF (very high frequency), and UHF (ultra-high frequency) refer to frequencies of 3–30 MHz, 30–300 MHz, and 300–3000 MHz (3 GHz), respectively. Radar engineers usually subdivide the UHF region above 1 GHz into "bands," e.g., L band (1–2 GHz) and S band (2–4 GHz). "Microwave radar" is a catch-all term for radars operating above approximately 600 MHz.

3. Cruise missiles are inherently difficult to detect by radar because of their small size (length approximately 20 feet, cross-sectional area of body approximately 2.4 square feet, wing span approximately 8.5 feet, weight approximately 3,000 pounds). Cruise missile infrared and acoustic emissions are also small compared with larger aircraft. This is largely because they are powered by very efficient miniature turbofan engines; the eight engines on a B-52H can produce 136,000 pounds of thrust, whereas a cruise missile is powered by only several hundred pounds of thrust. Kosta Tsipis, *Arsenal: Understanding Weapons in the Nuclear Age* (New York: Simon and Schuster, 1983), chapter 7.

4. Thomas B. Cochran, William M. Arkin, and Milton M. Hoenig, *Nuclear Weapons Databook*, Vol. I: *U.S. Nuclear Forces and Capabilities* (Cambridge, Mass.: Ballinger, 1984), p. 178. These authors base their estimate on DoD testimony at a Congressional hearing (Senate Armed Services Committee, FY 1981, Part 2, p. 50). Other analysts have speculated that cruise missile cross sections could be much lower.

5. Typical is a report that speculated that the B-2 frontal RCS would be about 0.05 m². Malcolm W. Browne, "Will the Stealth Bomber Work?" *New York Times Magazine*, July 17, 1988, p. 26. Actual tests of the B-2's RCS have not yet been performed.

6. So-called "Iron Ball" paint, black in appearance, is a coating impregnated with a high magnetic permeability material that absorbs microwave signals. For more on this and other stealth techniques, see Martin Streetly, "Hiding from Radar," *Interavia*, November 1988, pp. 1191–1192.

7. "$2 Billion for Hangars to Keep B-2s Cool," *Armed Forces Journal International*, March 1990, p. 18; and James Kitfield, "Air Force Faces High B-2 Support Costs," *Military Forum*, November/December 1989, p. 17.

8. Richard DeLauer, undersecretary of defense for research and engineering, has said that the stealth bomber "is 'invisible' only to certain kinds of radar but is visible to many optical systems, to IR systems, and to low-frequency radars. On the other hand development and deployment of a comprehensive and effective air defense system against the ATB based on the above technologies will probably take the Soviets at least 15 years and entail enormous expenditure. At a minimum the Soviets will have to develop a genuine lookdown/shoot-down capability and upgrade their SAM defenses with some kind of effective optical system. A major purpose of the ATB program is to compel the Soviets to spend far more on air defenses than we spend on our bomber force."

Similarly, if forcing the Soviets to invest in new air defenses is the objective of the B-2 program, the prospect of a thoroughly stealthy cruise missile would be most cost-effective, according to William Kaufmann. See Mike Synar, Richard K. Betts, William W. Kaufmann, Russell Daugherty, Richard DeLauer, and Dan Quayle, *U.S. Bomber Force Modernization*, National Security Paper Series No. 7 (Cambridge, Mass.: Institute for Foreign Policy Analysis Corporate Press, 1986). Kaufmann notes that: "The principal value of a robust U.S. strategic bomber force is that it forces the Soviet Union to invest enormous resources in air defense. On the other hand, it is not clear whether the difference in the B-1B's and the ATB's [Advanced Technology Bomber, the B-2] respective radar cross sections is significant enough to trigger massive additional Soviet investment in air defenses. If anything might trigger such an investment, it would be the prospect of a thoroughly 'stealthed' cruise missile, the prospect of which in turn poses the question of how cost-effective bombers are in general versus cruise missiles."

Former Defense Secretary James Schlesinger says that the B-2 "makes obsolescent $200 billion worth of Soviet air defenses." Quoted in Jacob V. Lamar, "Will This Bird Fly?" *Time*, December 5, 1988, p. 20.

9. See Michael E. Brown, "The U.S. Manned Bomber and Strategic Deterrence in the 1990s," *International Security*, Vol. 14, No. 2 (Fall 1989), pp. 5–46, for an illuminating discussion of the B-2's costs.

10. Jasper Welch, "Assessing the Value of Stealthy Aircraft and Cruise Missiles," *International Security*, Vol. 14, No. 2 (Fall 1989), pp. 47–63.

11. The dead zone is caused by radar interference with the

airframe, or by very large clutter returns. AWACS uses the frequency shift of a reflected radar wave to distinguish moving targets from stationary ground clutter (Doppler processing). The frequency shift is proportional to the velocity of a target in the direction of the beam. Targets traveling nearly perpendicular to a radar beam produce very small Doppler shifts. For moving radar platforms like AWACS, these shifts cannot be distinguished from the Doppler returns that result from radar sidelobes (energy that spills out of the main beam in all directions) which intercept the ground.

In unclassified notes for a short course on air defense, former SAC Chief of Applied Research Frank Heilenday assumes that AWACS has a dead zone of about 23 miles. He scales AWACS performance by assuming that current radar can detect a 10 m^2 target at the radar horizon of an AWACS cruising at 30,000 feet (roughly equivalent to the detection of a large fighter aircraft at 240 miles). Such a radar could detect a one-m^2 target (a stealthy bomber like B-1B) at about 135 miles. The range against targets with RCS of 0.1, 0.01, and 0.001 m2 would be approximately 75, 40, and 25 miles, respectively. Thus in this model, targets with an RCS of 0.001 or less are invisible to AWACS. Assuming the target's radial velocity with respect to AWACS is 500 mph, its time under radar coverage is less than six minutes if it has an RCS of 0.1, and less than 2 minutes if it has an RCS of 0.01.

12. Frank Heilenday, *Principles of Air Defense and Air-Vehicle Penetration* (Washington, D.C.: CEE Press Books, Continuing Engineering Education, George Washington University, 1988), chapter 10. A vivid and detailed picture of the very sporty game of air defense versus air offense can also be found in this book. A notable example was the Israeli Air Force campaign in the Bekaa Valley in 1982. The Israelis knew the location of the Syrian forces, the characteristics of their weapons, and Syrian tactics. The combined use of surprise, intelligence, jamming, remote piloted vehicles (to spoof SAMs), stand-off attacks by radar homing missiles, artillery shelling of SAM sites, and low-level strikes resulted in the complete destruction of a modern tactical air defense system in less than ten minutes.

13. In fact, the Air Force recently announced that it was dropping a cruise missile detection role for its planned North-Central OTH-B, in the sector that would have had cruise missile detection in the "Skip Zone" of OTH-B East and OTH-B West as one of its missions. George Leopold, "Air Force Rejects Cruise Missile Detection Role for OTH-B Radar," *Defense News*, March 12, 1990, p. 41.

14. Because of diffraction, the radar beamwidth scales as the radar wavelength divided by the antenna aperture. The drawbacks of low-frequency airborne radar stem from their longer wavelengths and proportionally larger beamwidths. In contrast to a ground-based system, the size of an airborne radar antenna cannot be easily increased to compensate for the use of a longer radar wavelength.

15. Edward H. Kolcum, "Lockheed-Georgia Seeking Major Role in ADI Development," *Aviation Week and Space Technology*, May 18, 1987, pp. 126–127.

16. Philip J. Klass, "Four Radar Firms Vie for FAA/USAR Air Surveillance Radar Contract," *Aviation Week and Space Technology*, May 23, 1988, pp. 94–96.

Chapter 4

THE EMERGING TECHNOLOGIES OF AIR DEFENSE

This chapter outlines the available technologies for air defense. The increased capabilities of current systems, compared to the more primitive forms from which they evolved, are due in large part to the revolutions of the past three decades in digital electronics, the miniaturization of electronic components, and signal-processing capabilities. Rapid advances in materials science and electro-optics have also had a major impact.

Only the most promising technologies are considered here. Some rough estimates for the costs of particular air defense components are given, but a detailed analysis of the cost of a specific air defense architecture is not. The discussion is also necessarily limited to a qualitative description of each technology's principal advantages and disadvantages, with most technical details omitted.[1]

The technologies fall into two general categories—surveillance and engagement. These are not independent, since an engagement system presupposes the existence of some type of surveillance system. The surveil-

73

lance and engagement technologies are discussed in
terms of the air defense applications noted in Chapter
2.

Sensors and Platforms for Surveillance

Ground-Based Line-of-Sight Radar. Ground-based
line-of-sight (LOS) radars are technically mature, relatively low in cost, can be scaled upwards in power (unlike
airborne radars, which have size and weight constraints),
and have resolution sufficient to direct fighter-interceptors or surface-to-air missiles to within their target acquisition range. The principal disadvantages of LOS
radars are their lack of mobility (except for small, relatively short-range systems), and the limitations of line-
of-sight propagation.

LOS propagation from the ground limits detection of
high altitude aircraft (30,000 feet) to about 250 miles.[2]
An aircraft at an altitude of 300 feet (lower by a factor
of 100) could be detected only at a range of about 25
miles, since range scales as the square root of altitude.
Low-altitude aircraft could also use the masking effect
of ground terrain to reduce detection ranges further.
The short range of ground radars against low-flying
targets means that many radars would be needed to
form a continuous barrier. While the individual elements are relatively inexpensive, the total system costs
would be high because merging the radars into an
effective network would require many radars and land
sites, data processing terminals, displays, and a complex
data communication and management system.

On a smooth earth a line of short-range radars
mounted on top of 100-foot platforms would have to be

spaced roughly 50 miles from one another to provide overlapping coverage of targets flying as low as 100 feet. High altitude coverage would require long-range radars. The North Warning System mixes 13 long-range radars and 39 short-range "gap-filler" radars in an attempt to provide all-altitude coverage of even small RCS targets crossing a barrier over 2,000 miles long.[3] The total cost for this system is estimated to be $1.3 billion. Lower costs would be expected for barriers created in less severe and more accessible environments than northern Canada.

Ground radars provide little time for identification or engagement of low-flying aircraft. A ground radar with an unobstructed view that is mounted on a 100-foot platform can detect a target flying at an altitude of 300 feet only to a distance of some 38 miles. Since the radar can scan in both directions, the width of the surveillance barrier is twice the range. A low-altitude target such as a cruise missile, crossing a radar barrier 76 miles wide with a radial velocity of 500 mph, would be under surveillance for only about 9 minutes, and might not even be in view the entire time because of irregularities in ground terrain. Flying lower than 100 feet, it would be in view for only 6 minutes. The obvious solution to this problem—mounting ground radars on high ground—is not always possible, especially near the coastline. An additional difficulty is that, at long distances, a line-of-sight ground radar views targets nearly head-on, where radar returns are usually smallest. As targets approach the radar, viewing may be from the side, where the returns are larger, but this is still likely to yield a smaller radar return than overhead illumination of the aircraft's wings.

Over-the-Horizon Backscatter Radar. At an estimated $2.3 billion, paid solely by the United States, over-the-horizon backscatter radars (OTH-B) are the most novel and expensive items in current air defense modernization. OTH-B's most important feature is its ability to overcome the line-of-sight limitations of conventional ground radar. OTH-B works, instead, by "bouncing" its radio signals off the ionosphere.[4]

OTH-B transmits radio waves in the high frequency (HF) band from 5 to 30 MHz upwards at a shallow angle towards the ionosphere. Energy at those frequencies, instead of propagating into space along its original path, is refracted (bent) back to earth. The amount of refraction is a function of the frequency of the electromagnetic wave and the electron density. (See footnote 4.) At HF frequencies, the electron density in the ionosphere is sufficiently great to cause an incident wave to be totally reflected as if the wave were bounced off a mirror at very high altitude. Reflections from the target travel back along a similar path; they are distinguished from ground returns via the Doppler effect. The Doppler effect here is the shift in radio frequency of the return from a target as a result of the object's radial motion relative to the source. A familiar analog to this is the change in the pitch that is heard as an ambulance siren or train whistle approaches and then recedes from a stationary observer. A representation of the process is shown in Figure 4-1.

From a single site, an OTH-B radar can provide all-altitude coverage at ranges between 500 to 2,000 miles in a surveillance barrier 180° wide. OTH-B radar designs are driven by the need to detect small targets at long ranges. The resulting requirement for a very high-powered and narrow beam demands a radar that is massive in scale. At the OTH-B site in Maine, twelve transmitters operate simultaneously, each producing 100,000 watts average power with high spectral purity.

FIGURE 4-1. *Over-the-Horizon Backscatter (OTH-B) Radar Principles*

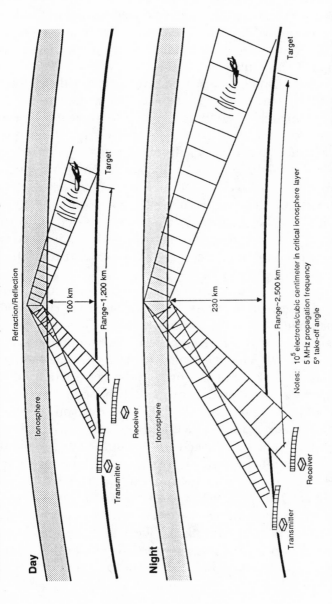

SOURCE: John C. Toomay, "Warning and Assessment Sensors," Fig. 8-2, p. 290, in Carter, Steinbruner, Zraket, *Managing Nuclear Operations*. Used by permission.

The transmitting antenna is some 4,000 feet long, and the receiving antenna is over 6,000 feet long. The need for a narrow beam for both adequate spatial resolution, and to limit the ground clutter returned in the radar echo, accounts in part for the extraordinary length of OTH-B's antenna.

The ionosphere consists of several electrically charged layers of extremely low density air at an altitude of approximately 40 to 220 miles (see footnote 4.) A radio wave propagating through this region is refracted in much the same way as light is bent at the interface of different media such as air and water. Higher frequencies are refracted less than lower frequencies (the amount of bending is inversely proportional to the square of the frequency). As noted above, for sufficiently low frequencies, or sufficiently high electron concentrations, an outgoing wave can be turned around by the refraction process.

The higher-altitude ionospheric layers also have higher electron densities. In the daytime, OTH-B propagation at 20 MHz may be reflected by the ionosphere's highest layer, the F layer, where electron densities are typically 10^6 electrons/cm^3. OTH-B propagation at around 5 MHz would normally be refracted back to earth by an electron density greater than approximately 10^5 electrons/cm^3, typical of daytime electron densities in the lower E region. Without the effect of the sun's ionizing radiation, electron densities fall at night. OTH-B must then shift its operation to lower frequencies to compensate for the reduced electron densities.

Since OTH-B in effect "looks down" from the ionosphere to the surface, it can in principle monitor the approach of penetrating bombers and cruise missiles even if they follow terrain-shielded, low-altitude flight paths. However, OTH-B must also contend with a ground radar return many orders of magnitude greater than target echoes. This is partially offset by increased target radar cross sections, which result from resonance phenomena when target dimensions are comparable to the illuminating wavelength.[5] However, at night, when the free electron density in the ionosphere falls, OTH-B must shift toward lower frequencies; as a consequence, performance against small targets like cruise missiles degrades.

Because OTH-B depends upon stable conditions in the ionosphere, it is subject to disruption in transitions from day to night and from season to season, as well as to outages following unpredictable events like solar storms. Naturally occurring small-scale ionospheric fluctuations can distort signals that pass through the irregularity region. As a result, operators of OTH-B continually make measurements of ionospheric conditions and adjust the operating frequency to optimize performance.[6] In general, the highest possible frequency is preferred, to reduce the effects of background noise and to reduce azimuthal beamwidths.

The dependence on stable ionospheric conditions means that OTH-B would be highly vulnerable to disruption in a nuclear environment even if it were not physically attacked. For example, a single nuclear detonation at an altitude of 50 miles is expected to have significant ionization effects out to distances of some 600 miles, and recovery could take minutes to a few hours.[7] Furthermore, OTH-B might be especially vulnerable to electromagnetic pulse because of its mile-long antenna. In addition, unless they are defended, the OTH-B antenna, control center, power sources, and timing synchronization system will be vulnerable to attack by conventional or terrorist forces. Since there will only be three OTH-B sites in the United States, the system cannot degrade gracefully under attack or disruption. Most observers, therefore, regard OTH-B as a peacetime surveillance system that would not be survivable in wartime.

OTH-B is being deployed in segments facing east, south, and west; OTH-B East, in Maine, reached operational status recently. The East and West segments, with 180° coverage, will face outward from sites near the two coastlines. Even as OTH-B becomes operational in Maine, options to increase its sensitivity by lengthening its receiving antenna to 8,000 feet are being considered. Other improvements planned for newer segments will also be retrofitted at the Maine site.

The geometry of OTH-B's propagation results in a 500-mile deep "skip zone" near the transmitter that is not under radar coverage. The Air Force plans to place a southern-facing radar in the north-central region of the United States so that its coverage will fill in the skip zone off the coast of OTH-B East and West, and cover airspace from Mexico to Cuba. An OTH-B radar with transmit and receive sites at Gulkama and Tok, Alaska, is expected by 1993 to extend the western OTH-B system further north. Ionospheric instabilities near the magnetic north pole preclude OTH-B operation in the Arctic.

Aerostats (Balloons) and Airships (Modern Blimps). Radars mounted on unmanned tethered balloons or manned rigid airships are a lower cost alternative for local area surveillance or defense, compared to aircraft-mounted radar like AWACS. Like aircraft-mounted radars, they have a low-altitude detection capability of relatively long range.

The United States already has some operational experience with aerostats. SEEK SKYHOOK is an aerostat that is part of the Joint Surveillance System for peace-time airspace sovereignty. Based off the Florida coast, SEEK SKYHOOK's primary use at present is to detect small aircraft carrying contraband (especially drugs) into the United States. SEEK SKYHOOK can carry an 8,000-pound payload to an altitude of some 12,000 feet. Its payload is sufficient to carry a radar capable of detecting a bomber-sized target out to its radar horizon of approximately 150 miles. Long-range detection of cruise missiles, however, would probably require a greater payload than it could carry. The United States is in the process of deploying a chain of aerostats along the southern border to aid in the interdiction of drug smuggling. The acquisition cost of these aerostats range up to about $20 million, including site preparation.

Airships would probably fly at lower altitudes than aerostats, and therefore have a shorter radar horizon, but their mobility would allow them to travel at slow speeds to different locations, and to take some evasive actions if attacked. One U.S. contractor has studied a design for a large airship with a volume of 5 million cubic feet. Its payload could be over 100,000 pounds, allowing the incorporation of very powerful radars. In addition, its size facilitates the use of large antennas, thus allowing lower frequency radars with better capabilities against small targets like cruise missiles.

The U.S. Navy is also considering the use of airships for fleet defense, particularly to ease concerns about high-speed cruise missile attack. While airborne early-warning aircraft can be used to establish a surveillance barrier, they are expensive and their continual use entails high operational costs. An airship could remain on station for weeks at a time. Early reports indicated that Navy officials were considering a 1.5 million–cubic foot blimp that would work in tandem with Aegis missile-firing cruisers. In addition to surveillance against aircraft and cruise missile attack, airship radars might provide command updates for Aegis-fired missiles. Each airship is estimated to cost about $70 million.[8]

Airship Industries was awarded a $168.9 million contract in June 1987 to build a prototype airship for aerial surveillance. Plans call for a demonstration airship, designated by the Navy as the YEZ-2A, to be a 2.5 million–cubic foot blimp that could remain on station for about a month. According to one report, the YEZ-2A was originally planned to carry a radar set from the E-2C airborne early warning aircraft and a new 40 foot by 10 foot internally mounted antenna, but these plans have changed to allow for tests of new radars being developed for the Air Defense Initiative.[9]

The chief disadvantages of aerostats and airships are their inability to fly in severe weather and, compared to aircraft alternatives, their relatively small payload capacity, increased vulnerability to attack, and lack of flexibility in deployment. For aerostats, there is the additional problem that the thousands of feet of tether holding it in place might interfere with commercial aviation should deployment occur near civilian air corridors. Airships pose less of a hazard to commercial aviation, and their maneuverability, although limited, gives them somewhat greater operational flexibility and survivability compared to tethered aerostats.

AWACS and Future Variants. The E-3 Airborne Warning and Control System (AWACS) aircraft is a much more sophisticated version of the airborne early warning aircraft incorporated into NORAD for continental air defense in the late 1950s and 1960s. Since AWACS was introduced in the late 1970s, it has seen extensive service in a variety of air defense roles, from airborne surveillance in the Persian Gulf to interception of Soviet Bear-H cruise missile carriers on training missions near Alaska. Although most of the 34 AWACS aircraft in the U.S. inventory are assigned to the Tactical Air Command, Air Force officials have said that in a crisis some portion of the AWACS force could be made available for CONUS air defense.

AWACS and similar, but less capable, aircraft like the carrier-based E-2C Hawkeye combine relatively long range detection with excellent mobility and ability to direct an air engagement of multiple fighters against multiple targets. The elevated platform of an AWACS radar allows it to detect low-altitude targets that might be invisible to ground radar; however, sophisticated Doppler signal processing is necessary to reject false targets that appear from radar echoes off the ground and sea.

AWACS was designed for theater engagements, incorporating features that reduce the visibility of its radar beacon to the enemy, and reduce the radar's vulnerability to jamming. Its major disadvantage is its high procurement and operational cost; a single AWACS costs approximately $200 million,[10] although a version designed specifically for continental air defense and procured in large numbers would cost less. To keep one AWACS continually airborne requires five aircraft because of the limited time the aircraft can be kept aloft and the need for maintenance. (Some analysts say the 5:1 ratio could be lowered to 3:1 for brief periods.)

The key question for AWACS and its future variants is whether their capability can keep pace with decreasing target signatures from stealth aircraft and cruise missiles since, as noted above, the attributes of radars best suited for small target detection are more easily incorporated into ground-based radars.

High-Altitude Drone Radar. ADI contract studies are investigating the potential for drone (unmanned) aircraft for wide-area surveillance at sites far from air bases. These studies are to produce a working design for a radar platform that can fly at very high altitudes—on the order of 60,000 feet—and remain on station for long periods of time. At 60,000 feet the visible horizon is approximately 300 miles, and the radar horizon is approximately 340 miles. Conformal radars (radars whose antenna are incorporated directly into the airframe) are being considered for these platforms in order to minimize weight and drag.

The long radar horizon of a very high altitude radar platform reduces the number of platforms needed to form a long radar barrier, and it also increases the time available to vector ground interceptors to their target. Drone radars might provide a cost-effective alternative to manned aircraft, which have less endurance and fly at lower altitude. They are also possible alternatives to OTH-B or space-based radar in layered air defense architectures meant to complement large-scale deployment of SDI. In the latter application, a chain of drone radars would provide outer barrier surveillance of Soviet bombers and cruise missile carriers, handing off target tracks to subsequent "middle layer" surveillance systems, such as AWACS on runway alert.

Designers foresee several problems with making drone radar a workable system. The aircraft's restricted payload limits its radar capabilities against low-observable vehicles. In addition, continuous operation would generate high operational costs, especially to replace drones lost to crashes, which officials fear would be more frequent than with manned aircraft. The problem of limited payload is shared by other proposals for very high altitude radar platforms, including high-altitude aerostats and high-altitude manned aircraft, and reflects the reduced lift that can be generated at high altitudes because of the low prevailing air density. Designers consider the development of drone radar a project of relatively high technical risk compared to alternatives like future variants of AWACS.

Infrared Search and Track Sets. All objects with a temperature above absolute zero (-273° C) are a source of electromagnetic radiation. Hotter objects emit more energy at shorter wavelengths, or higher frequencies, than colder objects. As an object is heated, it first emits most of its energy in the invisible infrared (wavelengths longer than the visible part of the spectrum); but as it warms further, it becomes visible, glowing red hot. An aircraft in flight emits infrared (IR) energy from engines, hot metal parts, and wings and control surfaces heated by friction with the atmosphere. The amount of energy emitted is a function of both the temperature and the area of the source. Aircraft can also reflect IR energy from the sun and the earth. The parts of an aircraft that are not heated may also be detected, in principle, as a cool body shadowing a warmer earth.

An IR search and track set consists of a collector of infrared energy (similar to a visual telescope), a detector, which may be an array of detecting elements, and associated signal-processing electronics. Ground systems can utilize large mirror optics to collect IR energy, whereas airborne systems are constrained by space and weight restrictions.

Like radar, these systems are able to search and track air-breathing targets. But the IR detector is easier to conceal, and is resistant to the electronic countermeasures typically employed against radar because it is passive; it only detects energy emitted by a target. In addition, the IR signature of a large aircraft is hard to conceal. Bomber engines emit thousands of watts of infrared energy, mostly in the short-wavelength infrared. Fighters are also prodigious producers of infrared energy, especially if pilots activate engine afterburners for high-thrust maneuvers.

The chief limitation of IR systems operating in the lower atmosphere is their short range. IR signals are attenuated by molecular constituents, such as water vapor, carbon dioxide, and ozone. Large fog particles, clouds and rain attenuate infrared radiation, primarily by scattering radiation out of the beam. Even in good weather, the range of typical systems is far less than radar unless both target and IR platform are at very high altitude, for example above 40,000 feet. Furthermore, although IR systems can detect and track a hot object, their passive operation precludes obtaining range information. For these reasons, proposals to use IR sensors for air defense usually envision using them as radar adjuncts rather than stand-alone systems.

Space-Based Infrared Sensors. The hot exhaust of a rocket booster is a copious emitter of short-wavelength infrared radiation that is easily detectable even from geo-synchronous orbit. Both the United States and the Soviet Union use space-based infrared (SBIR) detectors as part of their ballistic missile early warning network. Missile detection is possible because of the large infrared signal from rocket boosters and the absence of "noise" from earth background radiation or other naturally occurring phenomena at wavelengths where booster emission is greatest.

The absence of background radiation is due to the temperature difference of thousands of degrees between the earth's surface and the rocket exhaust.[11] In addition, the obscuring effects from localized hot sources on the ground, such as fires, can be minimized by operating space-based detectors only at infrared wavelengths that are not transmitted through the lower portion of the earth's atmosphere. By using the earth's atmosphere as a filter, space-based infrared detectors can look down at the earth and search for targets free of background, except for the potential problem of solar reflections from clouds.

In principle, aircraft and cruise missiles might also be detectable from space-based platforms. However, SBIR detection of air-breathing vehicles, even from low-earth orbit, is a substantially more difficult problem for several reasons, among them: the infrared signals are smaller by orders of magnitude, especially for cruise missiles; the lower part of the earth's atmosphere attenuates some of the already small signal; clouds or rain can eliminate the signal entirely; there is a much greater problem with earth background radiation; the detectors that are required to detect "long-wavelength" infrared radiation are more difficult to fabricate than short-wavelength detectors; and the detector must be carefully shielded from stray radiation, and its housing must be cooled to prevent the detector's own radiation from overwhelming the target signal.

The difficulties of space-based infrared detection should be contrasted with the problems discussed above for airborne infrared search and track systems. The background clutter problem is not nearly as severe for infrared search and track systems because they typically image their target against the sky, and not the earth. The sensitivity limits of a space-based sensor viewing a cluttered background are determined by the spatial and temporal characteristics of changes in the background, instead of the fundamental noise limits of the detector and its electronics.

A data base for SBIR is being built up by aircraft and Space Shuttle–based experiments that measure earth and atmospheric infrared backgrounds. Arctic regions are particularly important because they lie below probable bomber routes. However, regions where ice and water coexist may pose especially difficult background problems for practical SBIR detectors.

A "staring" infrared focal-plane array is an ideal detector for a SBIR sensor because it can monitor the movement of a hot object against a quiescent background. Each element of the focal-plane array images a small portion of the entire scene in the field of view of the collection optics. Target detection algorithms can then scan the output of a detector array looking for small differences in the ambient background that are consistent with the signal expected from an aircraft. Small differences in output that move across adjacent detector elements (which view adjacent portions of the real image) in a manner consistent with an aircraft's motion are one possible way to detect and track a target. Extensive on-board signal processing would be necessary for real-time detection and tracking of targets.

The theoretical performance of a staring array will increase as more elements are added. SBIR detectors of air-breathing targets are envisioned having detectors with hundreds of thousands or even millions of array elements.[12] Such large densities, presently beyond current fabrication capabilities, would be necessary to achieve performance levels that might enable detection of small emitters such as cruise missiles.

Long-wavelength infrared radiation is absorbed by clouds, rain, and fog. Thus, because of its dependence on favorable meteorological conditions, some analysts believe SBIR has limited military utility. They foresee SBIR, if deployed, as performing mostly an adjunct surveillance role, for example, providing coverage in the "nadir hole" of space-based radar coverage, or tracking aircraft flying above the clouds.[13]

Acoustic Detection Systems. A few tenths of one percent of the energy consumed by an aircraft in flight is converted to acoustic energy. Since acoustic detection is a well understood technology, analysts believe there would be only a small technical risk in a program to deploy an array of detectors as part of a surveillance system. Acoustic detectors, which are similar to microphones, operate passively, an advantage when enemy detection of the sensor is a consideration. In addition, acoustic detectors might be able to identify different types of aircraft by measuring their distinctive acoustic signatures. Their most likely application would be to augment radar surveillance systems that might otherwise be unable to detect low-flying or low-RCS targets like cruise missiles; acoustic sensors could provide valuable cueing information and rough target coordinates to reduce radar search volumes and increase radar sensitivity. In addition, an enemy air vehicle that feared acoustic detection might be forced to fly higher, where conventional ground-based radar performs better and has a longer range.

The primary drawbacks of acoustical detectors are their dependence on an acoustically quiet environment and their very short range. Even under good conditions, the range of a detector is typically a few miles or less. Acoustical detectors are sensitive to environmental conditions such as wind (if deployed overland) and sea-state (if deployed in water). This variability limits their military utility. Furthermore, although the cost of an individual sensor is low, many are needed for a network.

Operation and support costs would be particularly high in Arctic locations.

Acoustic detectors already play a key role in ASW, and might find specific application in detecting SLCM launches. Underwater acoustic arrays are being investigated that might detect the transient pulse of acoustic energy emitted from underwater launch of SLCMs or SLBMs. At present, SLCMs fired from submerged submarines are oriented and propelled beyond the surface by a rocket booster that ignites underwater. After broaching the surface, the cruise missile's tail fins unfold, the air-breathing engines are ignited, and the rocket booster drops off. Rocket booster ignition emits kilowatts of acoustic power, mostly at low frequencies. In favorable circumstances and in deep water, this signal might be detected hundreds or even thousands of miles from its source.[14]

Acoustic detection of launches from shallow water would probably be more difficult than deep water detection because of the unpredictable nature of sound paths in the seas near the coast. A SLCM launch detector would also have to contend with a difficult ocean background noise problem in this region. In addition, it should be recognized that in the future a responsive enemy could develop countermeasures to SLCM transient launch detectors, such as designing SLCMs to float to the surface with little acoustic noise and igniting engines outside the water to eliminate much of the low frequency acoustic transient.

Passive Coherent Location System. Passive coherent location system (PCLS) is an innovative surveillance concept that would use the radiation fields from VHF and UHF television transmitters, or FM radio transmitters, to illuminate targets flying within the borders of the United States (or any other nation possessing modern communications). A target in the vicinity of a PCLS receiver will cause an amplitude or phase disturbance in the received signal, much like the jitter that appears in a television picture when an aircraft or flock of birds passes near a receiving antenna. Target position could be determined by triangulation from two receivers; tracking would be possible with a network of receivers.

PCLS may be likened to an elaborate multi-static radar network. Such systems are potentially stealth-defeating, and they have the added virtue that they degrade gracefully if parts are destroyed. But commercial transmitters are not hardened against electromagnetic pulse and other nuclear effects, and therefore large parts of a network might be disabled following the detonation over the United States of even a single nuclear weapon. PCLS would, in any event, be useful only within the borders of the United States because television and radio broadcasts do not extend far offshore.

Space-Based Radar. It is sometimes said that space-based radar (SBR) is a surveillance solution in search of a mission. With its potential for world-wide coverage, SBR could have applications in continental air defense, theater air defense, battlefield surveillance, and ocean surveillance. Of the several competing designs for SBR, the one most frequently mentioned is a monostatic phased-array radar.[15] SBR would employ sophisticated Doppler-processing techniques to separate the small signal of a moving target from the larger background of ground or ocean radar returns; however, slow targets such as small propeller-driven aircraft might be lost in the clutter. The power requirements for the radar are a function of its altitude and the required sensitivity. Satellites that consume less than 100 kilowatts (kw) might be solar-powered. Higher powers might be met with nuclear power sources, although developing space-qualified nuclear sources raises a host of technical and policy issues. The National Research Council estimates that development of high-power nuclear reactors to supply space-based SDI weapons might not be available until 2030–2050, whereas the Pentagon estimates that such systems would be available between 2000–2010.[16]

Technically, SBR is considered a high-risk program. Among the challenges: designing a high-power, space-qualified radar with "superb" clutter rejection; developing fabrication techniques for the large antennas that would be deployed in space; maintaining the required stability of the antennas; incorporating substantial on-board signal-processing capabilities; and incorporating an identification system to distinguish hostile from friendly aircraft.

The satellites that would contain SBRs would also be considerably heavier than communication satellites. Estimates for the weight of a notional satellite are in the 10–20 ton range. Launch into polar orbit of a heavy radar satellite is likely to be accomplished with an expendable launch vehicle (ELV) taking off from the Air Force's Vandenberg Air Force Base launch facility. A satellite weighing close to twenty tons would require an ELV like the Titan IV. Launching a large constellation of space radars might very well strain U.S. lift capacity.

There are other problems as well. In a constrained fiscal environment, a commitment to build and deploy a constellation of radar satellites in space would compete for funds with the Air Force's existing commitment to long-range surveillance using OTH-B. Moreover, even proponents of SBR concede that the capability of SBR to meet an evolving low-observable threat is doubtful, given the problem of ground clutter and the constraints of long-range operation from high orbiting platforms. SBR detection capabilities in the near term are said to be for not smaller than fighter-sized aircraft.[17] In addition, designers are not optimistic that SBR could be used for both air defense and BMD. The problem is to design a radar that is suitable for both surveillance and tracking, traditionally seen as technically incompatible.[18]

An additional barrier to funding SBR may be its vulnerability. SBR is not an enduring wartime surveillance system. In a low-earth orbit, SBR would be vulnerable to even primitive anti-satellite attack from ground-launched missiles (unless it were protected by a capable ballistic missile defense). Regardless of its altitude, it would also be very vulnerable to jamming. However, like OTH-B, SBR's survivability in wartime does not affect its ability to perform the peacetime surveillance roles of air defense, the most important of which is to provide warning of atmospheric attack. For this mission, the frequency of sensor outage and the capability to distinguish natural outages from those that are deliberate are more important than survivability.

Estimating the cost of placing SBR in orbit is difficult, as the cost per launch includes both fixed and recurring costs. A crude estimate for the cost of launching a Titan IV is about $200 million. In addition to launch expenses, the cost to maintain the SBR constellation must be included. While SBR lifetimes are said to range from five to ten years, there is great uncertainty in these estimates because SBR would be an exceptionally complex system, parts of which are novel in design.

Estimates of the cost of each radar satellite are in the $0.5–1 billion range. A constellation of about nineteen satellites would be needed to provide continuous worldwide coverage from an altitude of about 2,000 km. This number could be reduced to about ten satellites if the requirement for continuous coverage were relaxed to a level at which 90 percent of the gaps in coverage lasted 10 minutes or less. Relaxing the requirement for worldwide coverage would also reduce the required number of satellites. (One proposal for an experimental version of SBR envisions a constellation of three satellites in polar orbit for coverage of the critical polar region, albeit with gaps in coverage of about 20 minutes.) Such a system could be augmented with other satellites or combined with ground-based sensors like OTH-B to monitor all approaches to the continental United States.

Obviously, a satellite deployment that provided only polar coverage would limit the utility of SBR for such missions as fleet defense. Nevertheless, proponents believe that even a limited deployment of SBR would demonstrate its potential for global surveillance, and regard such a demonstration as crucial in gathering the necessary support for the system to go forward.

For a sense of what an overall system might cost, see Table 2-1 for a summary of some surveillance alternatives and their costs for an air defense perimeter around North America.

Systems for Engagement

Surface-to Air Missile Systems. Surface-to-air missile systems (SAMs) are ground-based rocket interceptors usually employed to protect high-value military targets from short-range air attack. Modern air defense SAMs have conventional warheads; advances in guidance systems have allowed elimination of nuclear-tipped SAMs, which required elaborate command and control procedures and encountered public resistance when deployed near civilian populations. Some obvious benefits of using SAMs for local or "point" defense include their concentration of firepower and their good self-protection against air-breathing attack. Their survivability is also enhanced by their potential for mobility. Although no SAMs of any kind are currently deployed in CONUS, they are an important component of NATO air defense. They are also employed in large numbers by the Soviet Union for strategic air defense.

A state-of-the-art SAM system is the U.S. Patriot (formerly called the SAM-D). The Patriot missile is a Mach 3 solid-propellent rocket that is guided from a ground radar unit until its small on-board homing radar takes over close to the target. The Patriot firing system is mounted on four types of vehicles. One carries a radar set for target search, detection, identification, missile guidance, and electronic countermeasures. A notable feature of the Patriot's phased-array radar is its ability to maintain surveillance while tracking multiple targets. The operations of the radar set are controlled remotely by a computer that is part of an engagement control center mounted on a second vehicle. Electrical power is supplied from a third vehicle. The fourth vehicle carries 32 Patriot missiles that are stored in and launched from canisters. All operations are unmanned with the exception of the engagement control center.

The specifications for Patriot are reportedly a maximum slant range (the line-of-sight distance between two points not at the same elevation) of about 100 miles, and a minimum operating range and altitude of 2 miles and 200 feet, respectively.[19] In practice, the actual range of Patriot is a function of its flight profile. At low altitudes, most of a missile's energy is expended in friction with dense air. This and the problem of radar clutter near the earth's horizon result in a maximum usable range for Patriot against a low-altitude cruise missile of about 15 miles.

The cost of a Patriot battery is approximately $100 million (including the cost of 32 missiles at $750,000 each). To protect a point target like an airfield, three to four batteries would be needed. To protect a city like Washington, D.C., a large and irregular shape, about eleven batteries would be needed.[20] An alternative to Patriot would be the Hawk family of SAM systems, which cost one-third to one-half as much as Patriot but are less capable and more vulnerable to electronic countermeasures.

Future air defense missions may require SAM systems to destroy low RCS targets such as cruise missiles. Patriot is thought to be very capable against today's non-maneuvering and non-reactive cruise missiles. Because it is a ground-based system, the Patriot radar could also be increased in power without much difficulty. Therefore, designers hope that improvements in the sensitivity of Patriot and similar SAM systems will be able to keep pace with the expected decline in target visibility. But the weak link in engineering improvements to present-day SAMs may be difficulty in achieving the very good clutter rejection in both the illuminating radar and the missile radar seeker that are necessary for low altitude operation.

Look-Down Fighters. The modern fighter is the only means to identify and, if necessary, engage distant air-breathing targets. Fighters like the F-14, F-15, and F-16 carry sophisticated clutter-rejecting, look-down radars and radar-homing air-to-air missiles, like the AIM-7 Sparrow with a range in excess of 100 miles and a shoot-down capability. Fighters also carry shorter-range infrared sensors and heat-seeking missiles.

Fighters serve a number of theater air combat roles that are generally perceived as much more important than strategic air defense. These roles justify their high procurement cost. The Air Force's primary air superiority fighter is the F-15; its cost in 1988 was close to $40 million each. Perhaps the most capable U.S. fighter is the Navy F-14, each costing about $43 million, not including its radar-guided Phoenix missiles at $1 million each. The F-16 costs less than half as much as the F-14 or F-15, at approximately $16 million, but it is a less capable fighter, and due to size and weight restrictions, it carries a less powerful radar set than the F-14 or F-15.

An enemy cruise missile carrier traveling at about 500 mph and detected at OTH-B's maximum range of about 2000 miles would be within 1500 miles of U.S. territory (reported to be the maximum range of the current generation of Soviet ALCMs) in about one hour, and within 1000 miles of the United States in about two hours. The cruising speed of a long-range fighter is about 550 mph, although at a greatly increased rate of fuel consumption the F-15 can travel supersonically for short periods at about 1,850 mph. The F-16 fighter, modified for long-range flight by the addition of external fuel tanks, has a no-wind unrefueled mission radius close to 1000 miles (according to General Dynamics). Still longer ranges are possible with aerial refueling. Therefore, even under ideal conditions and flying to its maximum range with no wind, an F-16 on runway alert near the coast might only be able to intercept an ALCM carrier when the carrier was no more than 1000 miles offshore.

In actual operation, the F-16 would not achieve nearly as long a range, and intercepts would have to be made considerably closer to shore unless the F-16 were refueled. Refueling places its own complications on fighter operations and could also slow the fighter from its maximum long-range cruising speed. Cruise missiles launched from a point even 1000 miles away would still be able to attack coastal targets up to 500 miles inside the border. Should the United States decide it is necessary to have a weapons system that can destroy ALCM carriers at long distances, it will have to develop weapons that travel much faster, such as the hypersonic SAM, or to deploy fighters on forward-based platforms at sea.

The advantages of fighters have already been noted. Their disadvantages include their high cost and the limited time they can remain on station. Volume limitations in the fighter and in its radar-guided missiles constrain radar performance. A key technology issue is whether the radar homing missiles that are carried by fighters can be designed to engage very small–RCS targets like cruise missiles. For all these reasons, it may be that none of the aircraft in current inventories is the optimal choice of a fighter-interceptor for air defense.

Armed Transports. Fighters are expensive platforms for air-to-air missiles. An alternative under study is the armed transport. Instead of high performance fighter aircraft platforms, the armed transport is envisioned as a large airframe, perhaps a commercial cargo aircraft or jumbo jet, outfitted with a very large number of air-to-air missiles. Designers have speculated that high-performance, long-range, radar-homing air-to-air missiles weighing only about 500 pounds and with a range of about 150 miles are technically possible. Command and control for the missiles could be provided by AWACS-type aircraft. Alternatively, if the extra weight could be tolerated, search and fire-control radars and their associated support personnel could be carried directly on the transport. In Barry Blechman and Victor Utgoff's notional defense, for example, a DC-10 airframe converted to an armed transport carries 100 air-to-air missiles, a powerful surveillance radar, and a team of eight controllers, each of whom is assumed to be able to run four simultaneous intercepts.[21]

Perhaps the main disadvantage of the armed transport is that, compared with the fighter, it is a specialized aircraft with limited utility outside of air defense. Should the United States make a commitment to active air defenses that could complement heavy ballistic missile defenses, then interest in the armed transport would increase. In terms of cost effectiveness, analysts consider it a close second choice, or even a first choice, for defense of CONUS close to shore. An air defense architecture that postulated a layered defense might assign the armed transport to the middle layer, for example, within about 500 miles of the coast, because of the limited time the aircraft could remain on station.

Long-Range SAMs. Several concepts are being studied for very long-range SAMs (or Long-Range Missiles, "LRMs") that could be based in CONUS and destroy targets even thousands of miles away. The example above of a fighter-interceptor attempting to engage a cruise missile carrier before it reached its launch point demonstrated the need for a very fast weapon. This is illustrated graphically in Figure 4-2, which also shows the timeline for a long-range missile traveling at hypersonic speeds. Such a missile could reach an ALCM carrier well before the carrier reached its weapons release point.

The Air Force and DARPA (the Defense Advanced Research Projects Agency) have studied the feasibility and design of an LRM.[22] However, many technical questions must be resolved before a practical weapon system

FIGURE 4-2. *Interception Time Lines*

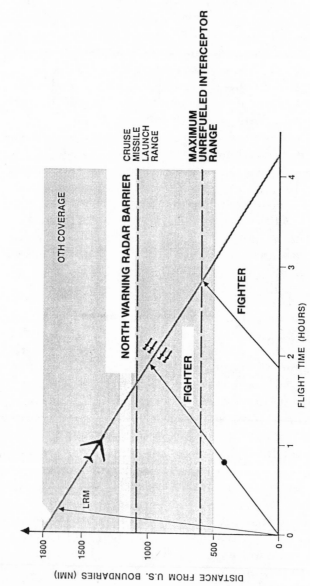

NOTE: The line from upper left to lower right shows the path of a cruise missile carrier and its cruise missiles after launch. LRM (long-range missile) notional speed 8000 nm/hour. Fighter notional speed 500 nm/hour. OTH (over-the-horizon) and North Warning radar coverage are shown for illustration; their coverages do not in fact overlap (see text). Cruise missile range and maximum unrefueled interceptor range are notional. The dot marks notional fighter refueling point.

could be developed. A key question is how to provide guidance for the missile to find its target, since a long-range missile is worthless without a long-range sensor.

Terminal guidance for a long-range SAM could be provided by a small radar seeker mounted on the missile. The job of the long-range sensor would therefore be to direct the LRM to within the target acquisition range of the radar seeker, a distance expected to be smaller than the acquisition range of a fighter because of the smaller size of the missile-mounted radar. The only system currently under development with a long-range search capability is OTH-B, and it is considered inadequate to this task.[23] Alternatives to OTH-B include: manned AWACS-type aircraft, perhaps forward-based on ships and flushed in a crisis, to form a long-range radar barrier that could provide guidance updates to an LRM; long-endurance drone radars, already being investigated as part of the ADI for long-range radar surveillance; or space-based radar. However, the ability of SBR to direct an LRM to within its target acquisition range is also suspect.

In a wartime application, the survivability of LRM bases and long-range sensors must be considered. Analysts usually assume that a near-perfect ballistic missile defense is available to protect these air defense resources. But especially vulnerable are those assets that are not proliferated, such as OTH-B and the LRM launch sites. LRM launch sites are usually envisioned as being few in number and located inland, so that an attack could not overwhelm any particular part of the CONUS border. Distributing the total number of missiles to only a few sites is also more cost-effective.

Practical problems with LRMs include finding ways to overcome the signal distortion that occurs when radar signals are transmitted through the intensely heated radome of a long-range missile traveling at supersonic speeds through the dense part of the atmosphere. The cost of the missile is also an outstanding issue. Should missile costs rival those of ICBMs (in effect, a long-range SAM is an ICBM on a depressed trajectory), the LRM would only be cost effective to engage cruise missile carriers.

The SDI and Applications to Air Defense

When the SDI was first proposed, some analysts imagined that the technologies envisioned for ballistic missile defense would also allow for a robust air defense. There are three general areas of possible overlap between SDI and strategic air defense: battle management/command and control, surveillance systems, and engagement systems. Near-term spin-off from SDI to air defense appears more likely in battle management or space-based infrared and radar surveillance than in engagement systems.[24]

Technologies being considered for ballistic missile defense as part of SDI include space-based interceptor rockets, space-based chemical lasers, space-based neutral particle beams, ground-based free electron lasers, ground-based excimer lasers, and electromagnetic launchers. The ground-based systems have a space-based component—relay mirrors in geosynchronous orbit and low-earth orbit—for over-the-horizon propagation. Although officials have said that defensive weapons will be nonnuclear, the feasibility of using nuclear-pumped X-ray lasers has also been investigated.

Of these systems, only ground-based and space-based

lasers operating at frequencies in which the atmosphere is transparent appear to be potential candidates for anti-aircraft or anti-cruise missile weapons. Interceptor rockets would burn up upon atmospheric re-entry. Space-based neutral particle beams cannot penetrate below an altitude of about 93 miles. The opacity of the atmosphere also rules out X-ray lasers for air defense applications. At present, free electron lasers and excimer laser weapons are very immature technologies. The possibility of developing useful weapons with them is sufficiently remote that they could not figure in the planning of air defense architectures within this century.[25]

Relatively little analysis has been published in the open literature describing the possibilities of high-energy lasers as air defense weapons. Perhaps the most comprehensive study to date was performed by Dr. Harvey Lynch, a physicist at Stanford University.[26] Lynch's analysis is consistent with technical analyses that have examined the utility of high-energy lasers specifically for the BMD mission. One of his conclusions is that if it is possible to design high energy laser weapons suitable for BMD, they might also be potent weapons against aircraft and cruise missiles. However, weather is a major uncertainty in the use of a laser weapon. Clouds and rain will severely attenuate and scatter laser light. Although infrared lasers can burn through thin cloud layers by vaporizing water droplets, propagation through thick clouds is unlikely. Dust and smoke can also degrade laser performance.[27] The lack of an all-weather capability thus detracts from the military utility of this or any similar weapon.

Moreover, an essential prerequisite to exploit even an ideal weapon is a target acquisition and tracking system. The problems of detecting, identifying, and tracking an air vehicle in the presence of the Earth's infrared and radar background have already been discussed. Furthermore, even in wartime, these problems may be compounded by the necessity to distinguish friendly from hostile aircraft. On the other hand, aircraft travel at speeds of only several hundred meters per second. Assuming a long-range surveillance system could be developed, an air defense would therefore have a much longer time to succeed in its detection and tracking mission than a ballistic missile defense would. The extra time could also be used to employ efficient "shoot-look-shoot" engagement strategies. The relatively small signatures of aircraft and cruise missiles and the relatively long time in which they are vulnerable to attack are similar to the problems and opportunities posed to the defender seeking to attack re-entry vehicles in the midcourse flight of a ballistic missile.

The obvious surveillance candidate is space-based radar. However, space-based radar could not provide the estimated one-meter tracking and pointing accuracy needed to attack aircraft. An antenna with a 100-meter aperture operating at a frequency of 1 GHz (0.3 m) from an altitude of 1000 km would resolve objects on the earth no smaller than about 2 miles. Tracking systems, perhaps based on infrared systems or laser radar, would therefore be necessary to complement an SBR surveillance system.

Even if the propagation and surveillance problems are resolved, one must consider what a responsive opponent might do to disguise or harden his air vehicle, or to disrupt, destroy, or spoof surveillance sensors. While the subject of countermeasures will not be treated here, it should be noted that the small signature of low-observable bombers and the even smaller signature of cruise missiles, offer intriguing possibilities to the offensive planner attempting to disguise these air vehicles or to create decoys.

The limitations imposed by weather, the problems of laser scattering and absorption in the dense part of the atmosphere, and perhaps most importantly, the target detection, identification, and tracking problem, have led most experts to discount the use of lasers for air defense. Those that do see possibilities concede that their utility is most likely as an adjunct to less exotic systems. The most frequently mentioned application would be to attack aircraft flying at high altitudes, since an aircraft flying in a denser part of the atmosphere or under cloud cover would be less vulnerable to laser attack. Note, too, that an aircraft flying through the lower atmosphere to avoid exposure to laser attack would still suffer the penalty of diminished range.

Notes

1. Some of the discussion in this chapter is drawn from presentations by participants at the CSIA-CIIPS air defense conference, supplemented by interviews, industry reports, defense journals, and standard texts on radar and infrared detection. A review of air defense technology that also addresses the repercussions for Canada appears in Daniel Hayward, *The Air Defense Initiative*, Issue Brief No. 9 (Ottawa: The Canadian Centre for Arms Control and Disarmament, 1988).

2. The line-of-sight (LOS) of a platform at height H to the horizon is $(2r_eH)^{1/2}$ where R_e is the radius of the earth. The LOS to a target at height h is therefore $(2R_eH)^{1/2}+(2R_eh)^{1/2} = (2R_e)^{1/2} \times (H^{1/2}+h^{1/2})$. This formula does not include a correction for refraction, which allows for some over-the-horizon radar propagation. A convenient expression for the radar LOS, including a factor of 1.15 to roughly approximate the effect of refraction, is LOS = 1.4 ($H^{1/2}$ + $h^{1/2}$) miles, where heights H, h are measured in feet and the value for R_e has been incorporated into the resulting expression. The

factor of 1.15 corresponds to the "4/3rds" model of atmospheric propagation, in which the radius of the Earth is treated as if it were 4/3 of its actual value.

3. John C. Toomay, "Warning and Assessment Sensors," in Ashton B. Carter, John D. Steinbruner, and Charles A. Zraket, *Managing Nuclear Operations* (Washington, D.C.: Brookings, 1987), p. 292.

4. The ionosphere is a rarefied region of the upper atmosphere where charged particles, created by the sun's ultraviolet energy, can exist in abundance. By some definitions, the ionosphere begins at an altitude of about 40 miles above the earth's surface, and extends as high as about 220 miles. Regions of the ionosphere vary according to diurnal, seasonal, and solar cycle periods. In addition, geophysical disturbances associated ultimately with solar variations give rise to significant changes in its structure. The electron density in the ionosphere is not uniform but, instead, forms a series of layers. The electron density generally increases with altitude, but within a layer it displays a broad maximum. The layers in ascending order of altitude are denoted "D," "E," and "F" (the F layer sometimes divides into two layers, "F1" and "F2," in the daytime under strong solar conditions). The rate of collisions between electrons and the surrounding atmospheric atomic and molecular constituents has an important role in radio propagation characteristics. In the D layer of the ionosphere, the electron density is relatively low because of frequent collisions with the relatively dense air. Conversely, in the more rarefied E and F layers, electron densities are high and collision frequencies are low. U.S. Department of Energy, Office of Energy Research, *Preliminary Environmental Assessment for the Satellite Power System*, Volume 2: *Detailed Assessment*, Report DOE/ER-0021/2 (Washington, D.C.: National Technical Information Service, October 1978), p. 149.

5. The radar cross section is a function of the illuminating radar frequency (or equivalently, wavelength, since wavelength = c/frequency, where c is the speed of light). Consider a perfectly conducting sphere of radius a. The circumference, $2 \times \pi \times a$, defines the characteristic dimension of the sphere. For wavelengths much longer than the circumference, the radar operates in the "Rayleigh Region." In this region the RCS decreases very rapidly, varying as the fourth power of the circumference divided by the wavelength. The (wavelength)[-4] dependence in backscattered radiation is characteristic of all objects that are small in comparison to the illuminating wavelength, and not just to spheres. (It can also be shown that in the

Rayleigh region the RCS is proportional to the volume of the scatterer squared divided by the wavelength raised to the fourth power.)

For the sphere, the peak value of the RCS is reached when the wavelength is equal to the circumference. The wavelength at which the peak backscatter occurs defines the "resonance" wavelength. For wavelengths shorter than the circumference, the RCS oscillates, gradually diminishing in value until it approaches the value of the projected area of the sphere $= \pi \times a^2$. Radar operation in this "optical" or high frequency region occurs when the wavelength is approximately 10 times smaller than the circumference. The peak value of the RCS for a sphere at resonance is a factor of 4 greater than the optical value.

The resonance wavelength for simple idealized targets such as spheres, ellipsoids, and rectangular plates occurs when the target "size" is comparable to the illuminating wavelength (here "size" refers to a one-dimensional size that characterizes these targets, like the circumference of a sphere), because the resonance condition is a standing wave phenomenon. Complex objects may be thought of as consisting of an overlapping series of these simpler objects, each contributing its own radar return upon illumination.

Consider the radar return from an aircraft. The shape of an aircraft is not smooth, and different portions may be in resonance with an illuminating radar. The return would be largest if the largest portions of the aircraft could be brought into resonance, assuming a favorable geometry for the return echo. Air defense radars that combine search and track functions typically operate in the 1–2 GHz region. Their wavelengths, 0.3–0.15 meters or about 1–0.5 feet, are much too small to resonate with the wings or fuselage of a bomber. Lowering the radar frequency would increase the RCS as the radar comes closer to operation in the resonance region. Unfortunately, lowering radar frequency significantly, for example, by a factor of ten to the 200–400 MHz region, forces design tradeoffs; lower frequency radars are larger, heavier, have large beamwidths, poorer spatial resolution, and are more vulnerable to jamming.

6. OTH-B also uses sophisticated Doppler processing to optimize performance and to distinguish moving targets from ground clutter. Signal-to-noise ratios are also enhanced by coherent integration with long processing times. Processing times are limited by target dynamics and the stability of the ionosphere along the propagation path. One to ten second integration times are reported to be

typical for aircraft. D. Curtis Schleher, *Introduction to Electronic Warfare* (Dedham, Mass.: Artech House, 1986), pp. 295–299.

7. Edwin Smith, "Nuclear Effects on RF Propagation," *C³I Handbook: Command, Control, Communications and Intelligence*, first ed. (Palo Alto: EW Communications, 1986), p. 205.

8. Alan Farnham, "The Battle to Build the Navy's Blimp," *New York Times*, March 22, 1987, Business Section, p. 1. See also "Drug Smuggling: Capabilities for Interdicting Private Aircraft Are Limited and Costly," GAO/G6D-89-93 (Washington, D.C.: U.S. GAO, June 1989), p. 36.

9. David A. Brown, "Airship Pushed for Early Warning, Mine Countermeasure Missions," *Aviation Week and Space Technology*, December 5, 1988, p. 65.

10. "Early Warning: DoD's Plans for Continuing Over-the-Horizon Radar Production," GAO/C-NSIAD-89-08 (Washington, D.C.: U.S. GAO, March 1989).

11. The earth's surface radiation can be modeled as an ideal "black body" radiator at a temperature of 300° K (80° F). At a temperature of 300° K, most of the emission occurs in a narrow band centered at a wavelength of approximately 10 microns. In contrast, if the average temperature of the exhaust plume of a rocket were 1500° K (about 2200° F), its peak emission would be near 2 microns. The amount of 2 micron radiation that emanates from a 300° K source is negligible.

12. Teal Ruby was a $500 million Air Force/DARPA program to place a cooled long-wavelength infrared staring mosaic array detector of some 100,000 elements into low-earth orbit. In an attempt to minimize the masking effect of the earth's infrared background radiation, Teal Ruby's detector was designed to measure simultaneously the thermal emission of bomber or cruise missile targets and that of the terrain, building up a large reference collection of IR signatures. Teal Ruby had been scheduled for the Space Shuttle flight immediately after Challenger, the failure of which in January 1986 resulted in a 2½ year delay in Shuttle launches and a decision to suspend Shuttle operations from Vandenberg, Teal Ruby's designated launch base. The long delay in Teal Ruby's launch and questions about its capacity to perform its mission prompted Congress to suspend all its funding except for storage. See Bruce A. Smith, "Teal Ruby Spacecraft to Be Put In Storage at Norton AFB," *Aviation Week and Space Technology*, January 8, 1990, pp. 22–23; and "Teal Ruby Funding Zeroed Out," *Spacewatch*, January 25, 1988, p. 3.

13. The nadir hole of space-based radar coverage is discussed in G.N. Tsandoulas, "Space-Based Radar," *Science*, July 17, 1987, pp. 257–262.

14. Author's communication from Theodore Postol, MIT.

15. For a technical review of SBR proposals and design trade-offs, see Tsandoulas, "Space-Based Radar."

16. R. Jeffrey Smith, "Panel Says Powering SDI Poses Major Challenges," *Washington Post*, January 19, 1989, p. 12.

17. "A joint Air Force–Navy space-based radar study concluded the technology is available for near real-time detection of fighter-sized aircraft. The study also concluded that a near-term SBR could detect, classify and track ships within a mile of their actual positions." *Military Space*, November 21, 1988, p. 4. The source for this report was U.S. Space Command head and Commander in Chief of NORAD General John Piotrowski.

18. Tsandoulas, "Space-Based Radar," p. 262.

19. Neville Brown, *The Future of Air Power* (New York: Holmes and Meier, 1986), p. 127.

20. A SAM system needs 360° coverage. The phased-array radar on the Patriot system will typically scan about 100°. Therefore, at least three Patriot units are needed for full coverage; four are necessary to have some overlap and redundancy. How many Patriots are needed to cover an irregular target like a city depends on the size of the area to be protected and the radar visibility. The most probable usable range for Patriot against potentially low altitude targets is roughly 700 square miles. According to William Delaney, Washington would require about eleven Patriot-type units.

21. Barry M. Blechman and Victor A. Utgoff, "Macroeconomics of Strategic Defense," *International Security*, Vol. 11, No. 3 (Winter 1986/87), pp. 33–70.

22. John D. Morrocco, "Push for Early SDI Deployment Could Spur Air Defense Initiative," *Aviation Week and Space Technology*, February 2, 1987.

23. The following statement from an unnamed Pentagon official in an interview with the Associated Press is typical: "OTH could detect planes at range and at least attempt to scramble fighters to find them. But no OTH system is good enough to direct ground-to-air missiles to a target." Cited in Norman Black, "Soviets Now Can Track 'Stealth' Aircraft," *Lowell Sun* (Lowell, Mass.), November 4, 1986, p. 8.

24. In a 1987 report, for example, SDI officials said that surviva-

ble communications and distributed computation could significantly improve air defense raid recognition, attack assessment, and assignment of fighter interceptors. According to the SDIO, a key ingredient in these improvements was the possibility of multiple sensor fusion—the simultaneous combination of information from multiple sensors operating at various wavelengths. *A Report to Congress on the Strategic Defense Initiative Deployment Schedule* (Washington, D.C.: Strategic Defense Initiative Office, May 12, 1987), pp. 13–15.

25. The technologies of BMD are reviewed in: Office of Technology Assessment (OTA), *SDI: Technology, Survivability and Software*, Report OTA-ISC-353 (Washington, D.C.: U.S. GPO, May 1988); *Science and Technology of Directed Energy Weapons: Report of the American Physical Society Study Group* (April 1987 preprint; final report published in *Reviews of Modern Physics*, July 1987); and OTA, *Ballistic Missile Defense Technology*, Report OTA-ISC-254 (Washington, D.C.: U.S. GPO, September 1985). Readers seeking further information from these studies should note that the OTA reports are more accessible than the highly technical American Physical Society study.

26. Harvey L. Lynch, "Technical Evaluation of Offensive Uses of SDI," Working Paper of the Center for International Security and Arms Control, Stanford University, Stanford, California, 1987, esp. pp. 8–25, 62–68.

27. This note highlights some of the considerations that would govern the making of a laser weapon. A high-energy laser could destroy an aircraft either by thermal kill (e.g., melting through the aircraft skin to ignite the fuel), the mechanism for continuous wave lasers, or by impulsive kill (cracking or tearing the aircraft skin and sending shock waves into the aircraft body), the mechanism for pulsed lasers. Laser damage depends on such factors as the laser power, the size of the laser spot, how much of the energy is coupled to the target, and the hardness of the target. These factors in turn are functions of the laser wavelength, polarization, angle of incidence, and surface composition of the target.

The complexity of the laser-material interaction makes it difficult to calculate, *a priori*, the threshold for laser "lethality." For lasers that propagate through the atmosphere, there is the added difficulty in accounting for absorption and scattering by molecular constituents, dust, and clouds, and the distorting effects of the atmosphere.

Continuous-wave (CW) lasers, like the prototypical CO_2 laser, may not be suitable for attacking aircraft because high power CW lasers deposit enough energy along their propagation path to cause "thermal blooming": as the atmosphere is heated along the propagation path, the density is reduced and non-uniformities (density fluctuations) appear in the index of refraction, causing the beam to distort and enlarge. Pulsed lasers avoid the thermal blooming problem but their peak intensity is limited by the onset of ionization; that is, for sufficiently bright lasers, the associated electric field is large enough to remove the outermost electron from an atom or molecule, thereby creating a plasma that is opaque to laser light. There are schemes that might work around both of these phenomena, but they would add to the complexity of making a practical weapon and they are themselves immature technologies that require substantial development.

Ground-based systems have essentially no restrictions on their size and weight. However, they require space-based relay mirrors to avoid the horizon problem and therefore they have long propagation paths. Diffraction causes an unavoidable spreading of the laser beam. If unreasonably large relay mirrors are to be avoided, ground-based systems must use relatively short wavelengths. Excimer lasers provide short-wavelength energy in the ultraviolet (0.3 microns, or if shifted by scattering in a hydrogen Raman cell to a more favorable atmospheric transmission wavelength, 0.5 microns), but their power levels are many orders of magnitude from levels necessary to make practical weapons. Free electron lasers are another potential source of short-wavelength energy, but many technical issues remain to be resolved before these systems could be scaled up in energy and function as useful weapons. The DF (deuterium fluoride) chemical laser is a relatively mature system, but its wavelength of 3.8 microns leads to unacceptable diffraction losses, or the requirement for mirrors of impractical size. Ground-based lasers will be large and few in number, and therefore would be inviting targets for SLBMs, nuclear-armed cruise missiles, or even conventional weapons and artillery.

The hydrogen fluoride chemical laser is the most likely near-term candidate for deployment in low-earth orbit for ballistic missile defense. Its wavelength of 2.7 microns is relatively long, but by deploying it in orbit the long paths of ground-based lasers can be avoided. However, to attack aircraft in dense parts of the atmosphere, the DF system would have to be used, which might also defeat fast-burn booster countermeasures.

If lasers are deployed in low orbit, a large constellation will be necessary to have a laser in view of all potential targets at all times.

Since aircraft can be attacked for much longer times than ballistic missiles, the number of laser battle stations could be relaxed considerably if the goal was only air defense, but a space-based deployment of chemical lasers that was not sized to handle the ballistic missile problem is improbable, to say the least. Depending on the assumptions used for the number of missiles that would need to be engaged, the time to engage each missile, and the battle station orbits, some 200 battle-laser battle stations might be needed for a chemical laser–based BMD.

The technical difficulties facing chemical lasers are discussed in a number of sources including the OTA and American Physical Society reports cited in note 25. These include developing scaled-up versions of the chemical laser, making it space-qualified, and providing it with an adequate pointing and tracking system. Vulnerability of defense assets in low-earth orbit to ground-based weapons or space mines is a major concern, as is transporting the fuel for the laser constellation. See calculations in Sidney D. Drell, Philip J. Farley, and David Holloway, "The Reagan Strategic Defense Initiative: A Technical, Political, and Arms Control Assessment," A Special Report of the Center for International Security and Arms Control, Stanford University, Palo Alto, California, July 1984, pp. 44–48.

Chapter 5

TRENDS IN SOVIET AIR-BREATHING FORCES AND THE IMPACT OF START

Much of the impetus for renewed interest in U.S. air defenses is a consequence of recent and projected developments in Soviet forces. The Soviet long-range bomber force is undergoing its first major modernization since the 1960s, so that by the mid-1990s most of the older bombers will have been replaced.[1] While the bomber has historically played only a small role as a delivery vehicle for Soviet nuclear warheads, this situation may be changing, and it now appears that the Soviets are moving toward a more balanced triad of nuclear forces.[2] The appearance of Bear-H cruise missile carriers flying training attack missions close to U.S. territory in Alaska is a recent development that is, at the very least, symbolic of renewed Soviet interest in finding an operational niche for their air-breathing forces.

This chapter reviews Soviet bomber and cruise missile programs, especially SLCMs (sea-launched cruise missiles), perhaps the most important new development in Soviet forces. Because ongoing arms control negotiations are likely to influence developments in these two areas, the chapter also outlines START goals and positions as of early 1990, and assesses the possible impact of a START agreement on these forces.

Bombers and Carriers

The current Soviet strategic bomber force consists of Bison, Bear, and Blackjack bombers. The 1989 Soviet bomber force is shown in Table 5-1. Blackjack is a new supersonic intercontinental penetrating bomber and cruise missile carrier that is similar to the U.S. B-1B.[3] Blackjack could carry a maximum of either 12 AS-15 long-range cruise missiles or 24 of the new AS-16

TABLE 5-1. Soviet Bomber Forces in 1989.

Bomber Type	Launchers	Warheads per Launcher	Total Warheads
Blackjack	15	12 Long-range ALCMs or 24 ASMs	180 or 360
Bear B/C/G	100	4 Gravity bombs or ASMs	400
Bear H	75	8 Long-range ALCMs	600
Bison	1	4 Gravity bombs or ASMs	60

SOURCES: Bonita J. Dombey, *Modernizing U.S. Offensive Forces: Costs, Effects and Alternatives* (Washington, D.C.: Congressional Budget Office, November 1987), p. 7; David Cox, *Trends in Continental Air Defence: A Canadian Perspective*, Occasional Paper No. 2 (Ottawa: Canadian Institute for International Peace and Security, December 1986), p. 15; *Soviet Military Power* (Washington, D.C.: Department of Defense, 1989), p. 46; and *The Military Balance 1989–1990* (London: International Institute for Strategic Studies, 1989), p. 33. For a slightly different assessment, see also "Soviet Strategic Nuclear Forces, End of 1989," Nuclear Notebook, *The Bulletin of the Atomic Scientists*, Vol. 46, No. 2 (March 1990), p. 49.

NOTE: In this table, ASMs (air-to-surface missiles) represent short-range missiles such as the AS-3 and AS-4, or for Blackjack, the AS-16. Backfires are excluded from this table.

SRAMs (short-range attack missiles).[4] Blackjack was first deployed in 1988; initially analysts expected a production run of at least 100. However, Blackjack deployments have been slower than expected. According to the 1989 edition of the Department of Defense's *Soviet Military Power*, fifteen Blackjacks have been produced.[5] Since the introduction of the Blackjack, an approximately equal number of aging Bison bombers have been retired.

A production line opened in 1984 for a cruise missile carrier based on the Bear H, a subsonic (0.8 Mach) turboprop bomber with an unrefueled combat radius of 5,000 miles. Some seventy-five are now reported operational.[6] By the mid- to late 1990s, the Soviet strategic bomber force is expected to consist of Bear H bombers, mostly converted to cruise missile carriers, and Blackjack bombers serving in both stand-off and penetrating roles. This force stands in sharp contrast to the mid-1980s force that consisted mostly of nearly obsolescent Bison and Bear bombers carrying only free-fall bombs. The Soviets also continue to improve what until recently had been a minimal aerial refueling tanker capability.

Cruise Missiles

An important recent change in Soviet air-breathing forces is the development of long-range (approximately 3000 km) air- and sea-launched cruise missiles, the AS-15 Kent and SS-N-21 Sampson, similar to the U.S. ALCM and Tomahawk.[7] The AS-15 is already fielded; the SS-N-21 is reported to have started deployment in 1988. A longer-range follow-on to the AS-15, designated the AS-X-19, is also expected. In addition, Soviet cruise missile programs are developing long-range supersonic variants including the SS-NX-24 SLCM, a large cruise missile that has been tested on converted Yankee SSBNs. Since the SS-NX-24 is too large to fit in standard-size torpedo tubes, analysts believe it will eventually be deployed on reconfigured Yankee class submarines or a new class of SSGN (nuclear-powered cruise missile attack submarine). The range of the SS-NX-24 has not been revealed publicly, but a supersonic cruise missile flying at low altitude might be limited to a range of only a few hundred miles. However, if published reports that the SS-NX-24 will fly at very high altitudes, say 60,000 feet, are correct, ranges in excess of those of current long-range subsonic cruise missiles may be possible.

The SS-N-21 is the first Soviet long-range SLCM. With a range of approximately 3000 km, it has the potential to attack the United States from ships or submarines stationed in the Canadian Arctic or far off the Atlantic or Pacific coasts. The Soviets emphasize submarine platforms for their SLCMs. This is also reflected in their arms control proposals.[8]

Potential platforms for the SS-N-21 include approximately two dozen Victor III attack submarines produced mostly between 1978 and 1985, converted Yankee SSBNs, and the newest and quietest generation of Soviet attack submarines, the Sierra and Akula classes. In principle, older submarines could also be modified to launch SLCMs instead of torpedoes. The Soviets have been slow in deploying SLCMs. According to some reports, their program is several years behind schedule, and in 1988 only four Soviet submarines were reported capable of carrying the SS-N-21.[9]

Even when program deficiencies are later corrected,

some analysts believe that operational constraints may still restrict the ultimate number of SLCMs the Soviets choose to deploy. Like U.S. cruise missiles, Soviet SLCMs (with the exception of the SS-NX-24) are designed to fit in a standard torpedo tube. However, possibly because of the hull construction of Soviet submarines, a vertical launch system has not been made an option, which will force a trade-off between torpedoes and SLCMs, placing practical restrictions on SLCM submarine loadings until dedicated submarine platforms are procured. The limited space on submarines is illustrated by the Victor III, which is credited with a load of only 18 torpedoes (six torpedo tubes) by *Jane's Fighting Ships*.[10]

The impact of operational constraints on Soviet SLCM deployments is only one factor that makes estimates of future deployments uncertain. In 1985, the Central Intelligence Agency (CIA) estimated that by the mid-1990s, there would be a total of 3000 Soviet ALCMs and SLCMs.[11] A breakdown of SLCM forces was not given, but based on the 3000 total, other analysts have projected a force total as high as 1500–2000 weapons. Lower estimates (500–1000) have also been made.[12]

The operational niche that SLCMs will find in Soviet strategy is uncertain. Soviet maritime strategy (unlike the United States) apparently does not envision forward deployments for their attack submarines, perhaps because Soviet submarines are noisier than their U.S. counterparts and face a sophisticated U.S. ASW force. Whether SLCM forces are envisioned for precursor attacks is also unclear. Before the Intermediate-range Nuclear Forces (INF) treaty, the Soviets had threatened to use SLCMs as a response to the U.S. INF deployment of short-flight-time Pershing IIs (viewed by the Soviets as a potential precursor weapon). In the past, the Soviets have also stated that they would use cruise missiles to counter a future U.S. ballistic missile defense.[13]

Possible Effects of a START Agreement

The prospective START treaty would reduce the strategic nuclear forces of the United States and the Soviet Union by about 30–50 percent to a ceiling of 6,000 nuclear warheads on each side. (See Table 5-2 for U.S. and Soviet positions on numerical limits.) Although ballistic missile forces would be cut by 50 percent under START, the proposal to count air-breathing weapons as less than their actual number would, in fact, allow both sides to possess several thousand weapons beyond the 6,000 limit. In addition, virtually all analyses of the START proposals have concluded that, even under an agreement, both the United States and the USSR would

TABLE 5-2. U.S.-Soviet START Positions (numerical limits as of February 1990).

	U.S. position	*Soviet position*
SNDVs	1600	1600
WARHEADS	6000	6000
Ballistic missile warheads	4900	4900
Sub-ceiling	3300 on ICBMs (prefers 3000)	3300 on SLBMs if 3300 limit on ICBMs
Heavy ICBM warheads	50% cut (to 1540)	50% cut (to 1540)

SOURCES: *Nuclear and Space Talks: U.S. and Soviet Proposals* (Washington D.C.: U.S. Arms Control and Disarmament Agency, January 22, 1990); Steven A. Hildreth, Al Tinajero, and Amy Woolf, *START: A Current Assessment of U.S. and Soviet Positions,* Congressional Research Service Report 88-400F (Washington, D.C.: U.S. Government Printing Office, June 1988).

be able to continue most of their plans for modernization unchanged.[14]

In addition to the warhead reduction, the United States and the USSR would reduce to a ceiling of 1600 strategic nuclear delivery vehicles (SNDVs) consisting of SLBMs and ICBMs and heavy (intercontinental) bombers. The two sides have also agreed on a limit of 1540 warheads on heavy missiles; the effect would be to cut in half the current Soviet complement of 308 ten-warhead SS-18 ICBMs.

Within the aggregate ceiling of 6000 strategic nuclear warheads, the sides have agreed to a sub-ceiling of 4900 on the combined number of ICBM and SLBM warheads. The two sides have also agreed that, as a result of the reductions, the aggregate throw-weight of the Soviet Union's ICBMs and SLBMs would be reduced by approximately 50 percent below the existing level, to a ceiling that would subsequently apply to both sides.

Limits on SLCMs have been a point of contention at the START talks. The Soviet Union has repeatedly expressed an interest in banning nuclear-armed SLCMs or limiting both nuclear and conventionally-armed SLCMs. The United States has resisted bans or limits for several reasons. First, the United States argues that SLCM limits could not be adequately verified without unacceptable interference with naval operations. Secondly, the United States is unwilling to accept limits on conventionally-armed SLCMs in a nuclear arms control treaty, both on principle, and because conventionally-armed SLCMs are an important element in U.S. naval strategy (the Navy is reported to be planning to deploy over 4,000 SLCMs on about 200 surface ships and submarines).[15] Finally, some officials are opposed to limits on nuclear SLCMs because they believe that nuclear cruise missiles enhance U.S. security. Some think, for example, that the United States can maintain its current advantage in cruise missile technologies. Others argue that cruise missiles could become an INF substitute for NATO and contribute to its retaliatory options.

The U.S. proposal for handling SLCMs has been for the sides to make unilateral, politically binding declarations of their nuclear SLCM deployment plans. The Soviets appeared receptive to this approach in February 1990, but backed away from it in April.

Of particular relevance to air defense are the counting rules that will be applied to heavy bombers and their nuclear armaments. Under START counting rules, each heavy bomber that is a penetrating bomber (i.e., not an ALCM carrier) counts as one SNDV against the 1600 ceiling and one warhead against the 6000 ceiling, regardless of the actual loading of gravity bombs and SRAMs.

For heavy bombers carrying ALCMs, a U.S. bomber will count as one SNDV against the 1600 ceiling, and 10 warheads against the 6000 ceiling. An existing Soviet bomber will count as one SNDV and eight warheads; future Soviet bombers will count as one and ten. Thus ALCM carriers will also be discounted below their actual loadings, but not as deeply as penetrating bombers.

Soviet Air-Breathing Forces in the Mid-1990s under START

The START counting rules provide an incentive for the Soviet Union, as well as the United States, to build up its bomber force and load it with gravity bombs and SRAMs. For example, a late-1990s force of 200 Blackjack bombers (admittedly, a number in excess of probable deployments) could carry 4800 SRAMs but would account for only 200 against the limit of 1600 SNDVs and the 1100 warheads that the Soviets are likely to deploy on the bomber force (assuming they deploy right up to the 4900 ballistic missile warhead sub-ceiling). This would leave 900 warheads to be allocated to ALCM carriers. Therefore, the agreement to count each existing Soviet ALCM carrier as eight warheads would allow 112 Bear-Hs and a total of some 5700 warheads on bombers. Still greater numbers of weapons are possible if some of the Bears are loaded with gravity bombs instead of ALCMs. It is easy to imagine force structures that, by taking advantage of the "discount" counting rules for heavy bombers, will increase the total number of weapons carried on Soviet bombers by factors of four to five.

Why has the United States encouraged a buildup of Soviet air-breathing forces, given the acknowledged limitations in the capabilities of NORAD and the existence of important military targets and large population centers near the long U.S. coastline? The most obvious explanation is that the United States is more interested in expanding and modernizing its own bomber force than it is in curtailing that of the Soviets. The B-2 bomber would count as only one warhead and only one SNDV against START ceilings, because it will be equipped with gravity bombs and SRAMs. Furthermore, given previous trends, some may believe that the Soviet heavy bomber force will remain small and that the Soviets will be unable to take full advantage of the bomber counting rules. It is certainly true that at the present time the United States is in a much better position to take advantage of the counting rules because of its larger bomber and tanker force, and larger bomber load capacity.[16] In fact, some SAC officials privately expressed surprise, if not delight, when the Soviet Union agreed to these bomber counting rules. (However, the uncertain fate of the B-2 may be tempering this view.)

In addition, the Reagan administration believed that a trend away from "fast-flyers" (ballistic missiles) towards "slow-flyers" (bombers) was in the U.S. interest. Historically, air-breathers have been considered second-strike, and therefore stabilizing, weapons. Whether the arrival of stealth bombers and low-observable cruise missiles will undermine this assumption is a key question for policy-makers.

The next question must be why the Soviets agreed to these counting rules. It might reflect their intention to build up their heavy bomber force, or it could reflect their belief that their air defense system has some damage-limitation capabilities against manned penetrators carrying short-range weapons. The limited capability of the U.S. air defense system also argues for START provisions that favor penetrating bombers over cruise missile carriers. The agreement to discount ALCM carriers less extensively than penetrating bombers might also force the United States to trade off ALCM carriers in favor of penetrating bombers. The Soviets may believe that their air defenses would be ineffective against cruise missiles. Limiting cruise missiles might also reflect their desire to remove some of the incentive for the U.S. program to develop and deploy advanced cruise missiles. Finally, the Soviets are believed to lag behind the United States in cruise missile technology.

In summary, Soviet forces are moving toward a more capable and balanced triad, as a new generation of strategic bombers and long-range ALCMs and SLCMs are fielded. START is likely to reinforce this trend because of its counting rules favoring strategic bombers and its absence of limits on SLCMs.

Notes

1. Testimony of Lawrence K. Gershwin, "Soviet Strategic Force Developments," before a joint session of the Subcommittee on Strategic and Theatre Nuclear Forces of the Senate Armed Services Committee, and the Subcommittee on Defense of the Senate Committee on Appropriations, June 26, 1985.

2. According to Stephen Meyer of MIT, when at Reykjavik General Akhromeyev appeared to make a concession on the counting rules for bombers, the Soviets had already decided to improve the air-breathing leg of their triad.

3. Blackjack is reported to be capable of traveling roughly 2,500 miles at Mach 2 at altitudes near 60,000 feet. Blackjack was not designed to yield the low observables of the B-1B, perhaps because U.S. air defenses were not judged significant. See Bill Sweetman, "Blackjack: Air Defense Challenge for the 1990s," *Interavia*, October 1988, pp. 1012–1014.

4. John Taylor, "Gallery of Soviet Aerospace Weapons," *Air Force Magazine*, Vol. 73, No. 3 (March 1990), p. 73.

5. *Soviet Military Power* (Washington D.C.: Department of Defense, 1989), p. 46.

6. *Arms Control and National Security: An Introduction* (Washington, D.C.: Arms Control Association, 1989), p. 155.

7. The present range of Soviet cruise missiles is thought to allow a launch in Arctic waters outside the range of the North Warning System ground radars, with landfall in Canada and the northern part of the United States. Longer-range variants similar to the U.S. Advanced Cruise Missile would allow the Soviet Union to target most of the United States.

8. David Cox, *Trends in Continental Air Defence: A Canadian Perspective*, Occasional Paper No. 2 (Ottawa: Canadian Institute for International Peace and Security, December 1986), pp. 20–22.

9. "Nuclear Notebook," *Bulletin of the Atomic Scientists*, October 1988, p. 55.

10. *Jane's Fighting Ships*, 1985–86 ed. (London: Jane's Publishing, 1985).

11. Gershwin, "Soviet Strategic Force Developments."

12. Daniel Hayward, *The Air Defense Initiative*, Issue Brief No. 9 (Ottawa: Canadian Centre for Arms Control and Disarmament, 1988), pp. 4–5.

13. See Rose E. Gottemoeller, *Land-Attack Cruise Missiles*, Adelphi Paper No. 226 (London: International Institute for Strategic Studies, Winter 1987/88), p. 28.

14. For example, see Robert Einhorn, "Strategic Arms Reduction Talks," and Walter B. Slocombe, "Force Posture Consequences of the START Treaty," both in *Survival*, Vol. 30, No. 5 (September/October 1988), pp. 387–401 and 402–408.

15. Paul R. Jaszka, "Multimission Tomahawk Employs Dual Guidance Systems," *Defense Electronics*, November 1988, p. 50.

16. The U.S. bomber force has nearly twice the number of bombers and three times as many warheads as the Soviet strategic bomber force.

Chapter 6

OBSERVATIONS AND CONCLUSIONS

Twenty years ago, Jack Ruina and Richard Garwin made the following assessment of continental air defense:

> Modernizing the [air defense] system to make it more effective against a Soviet bomber attack is very expensive and seems futile when one considers all the elements that make up the strategic equation—ICBMs, ABM, etc. Yet eliminating the system entirely is also hard to accept, since that would leave the U.S. wide open for the Soviets to get full use of their bombers and would allow any country to intrude in our airspace with impunity and perhaps without our knowledge.
>
> The dilemma of how to handle air defense is faced by our national leadership every year in one form or another as part of the budget cycle. Compromise proposals are generated, then postponed and then compromised some more. The situation begs for honest appraisals, and a conviction that a rational policy is possible. The money we now spend on air defense can serve sensible national objectives—objectives that are consistent with technology, costs, and needs.[1]

This appraisal remains appropriate today. Even as the current modernization program proceeds, the confusion over the missions of continental air defense is striking. Many of the arguments over the role of air defense in U.S. and Canadian security that were first aired when the system was substantially curtailed in the early 1960s have never been resolved. In part, this is a reflection of the ambiguity of some of air defense's missions, such as airspace sovereignty and "preventing a Soviet free ride." It is also the result of the tension between proponents of active defenses as a new basis for deterrence, and the large majority of analysts and officials who believe that mutual assured destruction is an inevitable consequence of the overwhelming dominance of offensive forces in the nuclear age.

This monograph has given an overview of the new developments that have led to a resurgence of interest in air defense. The most important new element in the strategic equation is the emerging threat from cruise missiles, and in particular, SLCMs. However, analysts differ sharply over the potential contribution—or the potential threat—that cruise missiles pose to U.S. and Canadian security. Until now, nuclear-armed cruise missiles have appeared to be a weapon without a clear mission. As a second-strike weapon that could be part of a reserve force, they appear to hold little advantage over swifter SLBMs. As a first-strike weapon, their role would appear to be confined to a high-risk precursor attack. Still, even an improbable threat will not be dismissed by conservative planners, and the possibility of a high-leverage attack is a threat to crisis stability.

The principal observations and conclusions of this review of continental air defense follow:

1. Soviet forces are moving towards a more capable and balanced triad with the fielding of a new generation of strategic bombers and the development of long-range

air- and sea-launched cruise missiles. START is likely to reinforce this trend because of the favorable counting rules afforded to strategic bombers, and the absence of limits on SLCMs.

2. In the competition between penetrating air vehicles and air defense, the advent of low-observable technologies and the inherently small observable signature of cruise missiles have given the offense a potent new advantage that will be costly to negate. Detection of even a stealth cruise missile flying over land may be possible with current technology, but only by adopting such brute force approaches as distributing a dense network of ground-based radars, acoustic sensors, or both. Long-range detection with airborne radar or ground-based over-the-horizon radar will require substantial improvements to keep pace with an evolving low-observable threat. The capability of over-the-horizon radar or future space-based systems to meet this evolving threat is uncertain at best.

3. The possibility of covert launch and the proximity of important military targets to the U.S. coastline have made SLCMs the most worrisome of the emerging air-breathing threats. An essential component of any effort to control this threat is the integration of a vigorous U.S. Navy anti-submarine warfare effort with Air Force surveillance programs.

4. The foremost mission for strategic air defense should be to provide unambiguous warning of an attack by bombers or cruise missiles. At a minimum, early warning sensors should provide the same 15–30 minutes of tactical warning as is provided by ballistic missile early warning sensors. The focus of the warning mission should be on protecting those parts of the U.S. deterrent force that depend on tactical warning to survive. In particular, warning is necessary for the survival of

the strategic bomber and tanker force and the fleet of emergency command and communications aircraft. In principle, many of these forces are vulnerable to surprise attack by cruise missiles. Planning for these forces today focuses almost entirely on ballistic missile attack.

Missile attack warning to the bombers could be disrupted, or the chain of command ordering ICBM launch under attack could be slowed, by a covert attack by air-breathing forces on missile warning radars and satellite relays or key strategic C^3 sites, many of which are located near the U.S. coastline. This small surprise precursor attack ("precursor" in the sense that the attack would be followed by a larger missile attack) is the most plausible attack scenario for air-breathers in a first strike. U.S. vulnerability to precursor attack would threaten first-strike crisis stability if Soviet planners believed that a successful attack held sufficient promise to blunt U.S. retaliation.

The precursor attack may be a high-leverage attack but it is also highly risky, especially when compared with the option of using the much faster SLBMs to attack the same targets. However, a covert attack by air-breathers offers the enemy at least the possibility of complete surprise. Like the bolt-from-the-blue missile attack, the air-breathing precursor attack might be very improbable, but its potentially adverse consequences on the capability of U.S. strategic forces to retaliate in a coordinated and effective manner might force conservative U.S. planners to consider changes in the disposition and day-to-day posture of strategic forces.

The United States could reduce its vulnerability to a precursor attack in three ways. First, it could make the targets of the attack less vulnerable by proliferating, dispersing, hiding, or making continuously mobile those forces and command/communication systems that depend on warning to survive. Second, it could develop new technical means to give prompt and reliable detection of air-breathing attack. Third, it could reduce the threat of a precursor attack through negotiations with the Soviet Union to control the threat from nuclear SLCMs. The multitude of technical problems for SLCM verification and the U.S. determination to retain conventionally-armed SLCMs to support naval anti-ship and conventional land attack missions make the prospects for an arms control solution to the SLCM problem uncertain at best. In the near term, the most practical way to reduce the threat of the precursor attack appears to be a combination of increased surveillance of cruise missile platforms, especially SLCM carriers, and the deployment of short-range ground-based detection systems, or balloon-borne or airship radar platforms at selected sites of high military value.

5. Although long-range nuclear-armed cruise missiles possess a sufficient combination of accuracy and yield to attack hardened targets, Soviet use of cruise missiles in a first-strike attack on inland targets such as U.S. ICBM silos and launch control centers seems unlikely because it appears to entail an unacceptable risk. First, long-range aircraft and cruise missiles travel at subsonic speeds and would therefore be vulnerable to detection for periods of time measured in hours. In contrast, Soviet ballistic missiles can strike anywhere in the United States in less than 30 minutes. The risk of detection would be especially high if U.S. military forces were in a heightened state of alert, as might be expected in a period of extreme tension. Second, an enemy planning to attack missile and bomber bases in the Midwest faces a difficult timing and coordination problem if detonations on widely separated targets are to be nearly simultaneous. The coordination problem would be even more

difficult if both coastal and inland targets are targeted. Finally, even if an enemy planner disregards the timing and coordination problem, the possibility of U.S. preemption during the time that forces are positioned for attack and weapons are traveling towards their targets could not be ignored. Nevertheless, if there is concern about this attack scenario, surveillance barriers in the interior of the U.S. could be erected, or short-range surveillance systems could be deployed along expected attack corridors and near SAC missile and bomber bases. The cost to provide warning to 200 high-value military targets would be roughly $5 billion.

6. Air defense's reliance on visual sighting by fighter-interceptors to distinguish friend from foe is an expensive, and sometimes impractical, solution to a problem that limits the capabilities of air defense systems in peacetime. In particular, the identification problem is a substantial complication to the air defense early warning mission, one that is largely absent in the analogous mission for ballistic missile defense, since ballistic missiles fly a trajectory that is not like that of any non-military vehicle.

7. The ground-based components of a damage-limiting and enduring ballistic missile defense would require a complementary air defense. Likewise, enduring air defense would require BMD at air bases, command centers, communication centers, and the like. However, in the near term, the impact of the SDI on air defense will be felt mostly in the areas of battle management, C^3, and sensor development, and not in the creation of useful weapons. Practical directed-energy weapon systems for air defense require capabilities and long development times similar to those envisioned for ballistic missile defense.

8. Canadian support for NORAD is being strained by

the U.S. commitment to SDI. Canadians appear ready to support the historic mission of NORAD, that of protecting the U.S. deterrent via "passive" warning systems, but fear that participation in defenses capable of defeating an attack ("active defenses") might draw them into superpower conflicts. Canadian ability to finance large-scale defensive deployments is also questionable.

9. Active-engagement air defenses are neither necessary to deter air attack, nor likely to contribute to meaningful damage limitation in the absence of either an effective missile defense or radical reductions in ballistic missile arsenals well beyond those contemplated under START.

10. Conservative estimates of the cost for a comprehensive air defense, of the kind that would complement a nationwide deployment of SDI by defeating the Soviet air-breathing threat of the late 1990s, range from $100 to $200 billion. One uncertainty in these estimates is the cost of a terminal missile defense to protect vulnerable air defense resources. The estimates also make optimistic assumptions about the performance of ballistic missile and air defense weapons, and they do not assume an especially responsive opponent.

A comprehensive review of all of the issues surrounding cruise missiles is long overdue. It should especially focus on the technical options to detect cruise missiles, the role of nuclear and conventional variants in U.S. and NATO strategy, the practical limits of cruise missile design, and the potential for arms control limitations (including an evaluation of verification technologies).

Notes

1. Jack Ruina and Richard Garwin, "Continental Air Defense," unpublished manuscript, March 10, 1970.

CSIA-CIIPS Strategic Air Defense Conference Participants*
February 12–13, 1988, Kennedy School of Government, Cambridge, Mass.

Kerry Abelson
Pre-doctoral fellow, CSIA

John Anderson
Former Assistant Deputy
    Minister (Policy),
    Department of National
    Defence, Canada

Brig. Gen. James Andrus
Director of NORAD
    Planning Staff

Maj. Gen. Neil Beer (USAF,
    ret.), President, Western
    Research Corp.

Jane Boulden
Queens University, Canada

Dave Briggs
Associate Head, Surveillance
    and Control Division, MIT
    Lincoln Laboratory

Lt. Gen. Bruce K. Brown
    (USAF, ret.), The BDM
    Corporation

Michael Bryans
Editor, CIIPS

Ashton B. Carter
Associate Director, CSIA

Art Charo
Conference Coordinator;
    Sloan Foundation
    Research Fellow, CSIA

Antonia Handler Chayes
Former Undersecretary of
    the Air Force;
    Chairperson, EnDispute,
    Inc.

Lt. Col. Gary Clay
Director of Air Plans,
    National Defence HQ,
    Canada

*affiliation at time of conference

Jim Moore
Operations Research and
  Analysis Establishment,
  Department of National
  Defense, Canada

Sofia Mortada
CSIA Staff

Joseph S. Nye, Jr.
Director, CSIA

Geoffrey Pearson
Executive Director, CIIPS

Ted Postol
Center for International
  Security and Arms
  Control, Stanford
  University

Ron Purver
Research Associate, CIIPS

Arthur Pyrak
Chief of Air Defense
  Branch, CIA

Douglas Ross
Department of Political
  Science, University of
  British Columbia, Canada

Jack Ruina
Director, Defense and Arms
  Control Studies Program,
  Center for International
  Studies, MIT

Peter Sharfman
Program Manager,
  International Security and
  Commerce, U.S.
  Congressional Office of
  Technology Assessment

Ron Stansfield
Head, Nuclear Affairs,
  Defence Relations
  Division, Department of
  External Affairs, Canada

Victor Utgoff
Institute for Defense
  Analyses

Maj. Gen. Jasper Welch
  (USAF, ret.)
Jasper Welch Associates

Col. Bill Weston
Director of Public Policy,
  Department of National
  Defense, Canada

Lynn Whittaker
Director of Programs and
  Publications, CSIA

Lawrence Woodruff
Deputy Undersecretary of
  Defense for Strategic and
  Theater Nuclear Forces

Charles Zraket
President and CEO, The
  MITRE Corporation

ACRONYM LIST

AACE	Aircraft Alerting Communications EMP [system]
ABM	anti–ballistic missile
ACM	Advanced Cruise Missile
ADI	Air Defense Initiative
ALCM	air-launched cruise missile
AMRAAM	Advanced Medium Range Air-to-Air Missile
ANG	Air National Guard
ASM	air-to-surface missile
ASTS	Advanced Surveillance and Tracking System
ASTT	Advanced Surveillance Tracking and Technologies
ASW	anti-submarine warfare
ATB	Advanced Technology Bomber [B-2]
AWACS	Airborne Warning and Control System
BMD	ballistic missile defense
BMEWS	ballistic missile early warning system
C^2	command and control
C^3	command, control, and communications
C^3I	command, control, communication, and intelligence
CIA	Central Intelligence Agency
CINC	Commander-in-Chief
CINCEUR	Commander-in-Chief, Europe
CINCLANT	Commander-in-Chief, Atlantic
CINCPAC	Commander-in-Chief, Pacific

CINCSAC	Commander-in-Chief, Strategic Air Command
CONUS	Continental United States
CW	continuous-wave [laser]
DARPA	Defense Advanced Research Projects Agency
DEW	Distant Early Warning [radars]
DF	deuterium fluoride [lasers]
DoD	Department of Defense
ECCM	electronic counter-countermeasures
ECM	electronic countermeasures
ELV	expendable launch vehicle
EMP	electro-magnetic pulse
ERIS	exo-atmospheric intercept system
FAA	Federal Aviation Administration
FY	fiscal year
GHz	gigahertz
GPS	Global Positioning Satellite
GWEN	Ground-Wave Emergency Network
HASC	House Armed Services Committee
HEDI	high-altitude endo-atmospheric intercept [missile]
HF	high frequency
ICBM	intercontinental ballistic missile
IFF	identification friend-or-foe
INF	Intermediate-range Nuclear Forces
IR	infrared
JSS	Joint Surveillance System
JUSCADS	Joint U.S.-Canadian Air Defense Study
LOS	line-of-sight
LRM	long-range missile
LUA	launch under attack
MAD	mutually assured destruction
MAR	minimally attended radar
MHz	megahertz
MIRV	multiple independently-targetable reentry vehicle
MX	Missile Experimental [Peacekeeper]
NATO	North Atlantic Treaty Organization

NCA	National Command Authority
NDS	Nuclear Detonation System
NEACP	National Emergency Airborne Command Post
nm	nautical miles
NORAD	North American Aerospace Defense Command [formerly North American Air Defense Command]
NSDM	National Security Decision Memorandum
NWS	North Warning System
OSD	Office of the Secretary of Defense
OTA	Office of Technology Assessment
OTH-B	over-the-horizon backscatter [radar]
PACCS	Post-Attack Command and Control System
PAL	permissive action link
PARCS	Perimeter Acquisition Radar Control System
PCL	positive control launch
PCLS	passive coherence location system
PD	Presidential Directive
RAM	radar-absorbing material
RCAF	Royal Canadian Air Force
RCS	radar cross-section
ROCC	Region Operations Control Center
RPV	remotely piloted vehicle
SAC	Strategic Air Command
SAGE	Semi-Automatic Ground Environment [computer-controlled radar network]
SALT	Strategic Arms Limitation Talks
SAM	surface-to-air missile
SASC	Senate Armed Services Committee
SBIR	space-based infrared [detector]
SBR	space-based radar
SDI	Strategic Defense Initiative
SDIO	SDI Organization
SEWS	satellite early warning system
SIOP	Single Integrated Operational Plan [the U.S. nuclear war plan]
SLBM	submarine-launched ballistic missile

SLCM	sea-launched cruise missile
SNDV	strategic nuclear delivery vehicles
SRAM	short-range attack missile
SSBN	sub-surface, ballistic, nuclear [nuclear-powered ballistic-missile submarine]
SSGN	nuclear-powered cruise (guided) missile attack submarine
SSN	sub-surface nuclear (nuclear-powered attack submarine)
START	Strategic Arms Reduction Talks
TAC	Tactical Air Command
TACAMO	"take charge and move out" [submarine-communication relay aircraft]
TW	tactical warning
UAR	unattended radar
UHF	ultra high frequency
USAF	United States Air Force
U.S. GAO	U.S. Government Accounting Office
U.S. GPO	U.S. Government Printing Office
VHF	very high frequency
VLF	very low frequency
WWABNCP	Worldwide Airborne Nuclear Command Post

INDEX